BullyProof Yourself At Work!

Personal Strategies to Stop the Hurt From Harassment

Gary Namie, Ph.D.
and
Ruth Namie, Ph.D.

Illustrated by Mark Hughes

DoubleDoc Press
A Division of The Work Doctor ®
Benicia, California

BullyProof Yourself At Work!

Personal Strategies to Stop the Hurt From Harassment
by Gary Namie, Ph.D. and Ruth Namie, Ph.D.

DoubleDoc Press

A Division of The Work Doctor®
Post Office Box 761
Benicia, California 94510 U.S.A.
707.745.6630

Illustrations by Mark Hughes at
The Cartoon Factory, Burlington, VT (802) 863-5374
Cover design by Patson's Press (Remarque Loy), Sunnyvale, CA
The Work Doctor is a registered trademark of Gary Namie

Publisher's Catologing-in-Publication
Namie, Gary
   BullyProof yourself at work! : personal
strategies to stop the hurt from harassment
Gary Namie and Ruth Namie. -- 1st ed.

   p. cm.
   Includes bibiographical references and index.
   Includes index.
   LCCN: 98-96836
   ISBN: 0-9668629-5-3

   1. Bullying in the workplace. 2. Managing your
boss. 3. Office politics. I. Namie, Ruth. II.
Title.

HF5548.83.N36 1999   650.1'3
                                QB198-1768

Printed in the United States of America

In the memory of
Lillian and Florence
and to Pat,
the three women
who always gave
unconditional love
and support.

Each time a man stands up for an ideal,
or acts to improve the lot of others, or strikes
out against injustice, he sends forth a tiny
ripple of hope, and crossing each other from a
million different centers of energy and daring,
those ripples build a current which can sweep
down the mightiest walls of oppression and injustice.

- Robert F. Kennedy

Contents

Section Three: Moving On, Up or Out

Acknowledgment

Some of the most beautiful things in Nature are the giant Sequoia and Redwood trees that grow in Ruth's native California. Nature, in her wisdom, only allows new growth of these trees to come from destruction of the seed pod by fire. It was through personal destruction and pain our cause was born.

At the top of the list to thank are the thousands of anonymous people who visit with us virtually at the web site or by telephone to share their stories, seek advice or support. They, in turn, launched the U.S. anti-bullying movement with their sacrifices.

Special thanks go to Daniel Levine, Employee Advocate extraordinaire and Gary Purece for his insights. We are blessed with experts who encourage the introduction of bullying to the U.S. — Andy Ellis, Susan Marais-Steinman, and Tim Field from overseas and our academic advisors, Loraleigh Keashly and David Yamada. Mindy Werner-Crohn, MD, June Chewning, and Carol Fehner help in special ways beyond description. April Harper, Australian eagle eye and advocate, improved the text with her insightful, sensitizing comments.

We acknowledge the support of those closest and dearest to our hearts. The two Helens, Helen Williams who has been with us since the beginning and Helen King whose invaluable assistance was appreciated, and our children, Macario Namie, Sean Lunsford, Robyn and Sumiko California.

Finally, thanks for the steadfast love from Ike Namie. He made the Campaign, the book series and the future all possible.

Introduction

A simple truth: to stop a bully from turning you into a Target, **just** firmly announce that her behavior (when she decides to test your resistance) will not be accepted without her running the risk that it will be reported immediately to both a private lawyer and the company's legal team. Gesture that she has one chance to stop now (palm of your raised hand facing her) and that she consider the consequences of continuing her childish, embarrassing behavior.

Easy to say, right? Easy to understand and dream about, too. But nearly impossible to do. If it were *just that simple,* you would have done it in the first place and skipped all the misery from being the bully's Target.

All the pain now felt comes not from that single missed opportunity alone, but from the postponement of taking action to right the wrong. Nipping it in the bud, people call it. But using another old saying, *it's all water under the bridge,* the current situation requires you to stop the hurt now however you can.

That is the reason for this book in The Work Doctor's Bullying Series.

BullyProofing Comes First

Based on the thousands of individuals we have coached and met through the first internet site in the U.S. dedicated to Workplace Bullying, we at The Work Doctor developed a two-phase approach for individuals that can restore self-respect and dignity at work.

Phase 1: Personal Strategies for BullyProofing —
what one individual can do to minimize hurt.

and

Phase 2: BullyBusting (with a little help from friends) —
previewed in the last two chapters of this book.

By first becoming proficient at BullyProofing yourself, you can prevent the bully from getting inside your head, of convincing you that lies are truths. Going to work need not jeopardize your health.

Once BullyProofed, you then have to decide how to get the bully off your back now and forever. Some people are ready to begin bringing the bully down when first assaulted because they were more enraged than wounded. This does not make them superior, smarter, stronger, better, or more valuable. Those rare birds simply have a different way of responding to nasty, brutal attackers.

Caution: if you are not one of those who can go directly to Phase 2 (and most of us are not), do not try to take action while still vulnerable or reeling from assaults from the bully. If you do, you will most probably fail. There is a time to counterattack and a time to heal.

Phase 1 is about regrouping, healing, and retaking what was stolen from you—self-confidence, the belief in your competence and goodness. BullyProofing can be accomplished alone or with trusted family and friends. It does not require a public commitment to action.

Phase 2 is the assertive, public reclaiming of your dignity at work. You will need all the energy your mind and soul can muster to rid the workplace of the creep who makes life miserable for you.

After BullyProofing yourself, you are less likely to be a future Target.

Sacrifice Health &Sanity For A Paycheck? It Simply Doesn't Add Up

Understanding BullySpeak

BullySpeak, is a vocabulary that we deliberately choose to use so that we neither offend crusaders for other social justice causes nor confuse the employees we attempt to reach through the Campaign Against Workplace Bullying.

Key features of the jargon:

Targets and bullies
Out of respect to Targets, with whom we sympathize, and disrespect for bullies, who deserve no praise, we always capitalize Targets and only begrudgingly capitalize bullies if the word happens to begin a sentence.

Targets merely had the bad fortune to run into a bully too lazy to acknowledge and work through her personal list of deficiencies. A Targets drifts in, and hopefully out of, the crosshairs of the bully's scope.

Female is the preferred gender
We use the pronoun "she" throughout the text to describe both the Target, the recipient of mistreatment at work, and the bully, the perpetrator. We need to expand harassment's definitional boundaries beyond the narrow protected class EEO categories of female, minority, older, disabled workers. Also, the majority of advice seekers who contact us are women who are stalked by women bullies. We are not ignoring men. They only have to make

mental pronoun substitutions throughout the text. They need only ask a woman for help; she's been doing it for a lifetime.

Targets, not victims

Bullies select Targets to harm. Targets are recipients of unrelenting verbal assaults that cut to the core of the Target's being. Over time, the Target's personality gets trampled. When Targets see themselves as victims, two undesirable things can happen:

- if they have a personal history of being exploited by others in their family or in other relationships, victimhood lures them back to a painful time. Once there, victims find it harder to act to reverse their situation.

- victimhood begets powerlessness, helplessness, and an inability to change matters for the better.

Bullying, not abuse

Abusers have victims. Battered spouses and children deserve to have the terms abuse and victim reserved for them because they suffer physical violence unlike Targets of bullying. Workplace bullying involves abuse of power, but we shy away from using the term abuse whenever possible.

Cheerleaders for corporate competition are quick to denigrate victims as deserving their fate. Wrong! Bullied Targets no more like the torment they endure than rape victims are likely to seek out the rapist. The anti-bullying movement is not asking for pity from the morally bankrupt.

Folks in Britain coined the phrase "workplace bullying." So it should be good enough for us Americans. It is instantly recognizable. Every time we stand in line at a store, sit at an airport, or talk to a reporter we get to hear someone's memory of torment at work, either theirs or a friend's. It is that common, a "silent epidemic" ready to be pushed into the light of day (or press and media scrutiny as light is defined in the modern world).

Targets Don't Deserve Or Want What They Get. Bullies Are Liars & Cowards!

How the Book is Organized

- **Section One: The Silent Epidemic Exposed**
  These chapters define Workplace Bullying. We introduce the players—bullies, the bully perpetrator, and Targets, the recipients. Next comes critical information to help you, and others who care about you, identify the price for bullying paid by Targets. Taken together, these chapters ensure you, your family and colleagues that the unjust bullying situation is not of your own making.

  Chapter 4 describes the simple, yet profound, reason why bullies and Targets are who they are. We attempt to answer why Targets seem doomed to eternal head-scratching bafflement and hurt when facing a bully. This is the answer to many of the "why" questions.

  Fear prevents both Targets and witnesses from taking action against the bully. Several reasons are given.

Chapter 6 is a "consumer's guide" for Targets needing help from others to choose carefully from those offering support. Family and friends wishing to support the Target can learn here the best ways to do it.

- ## Section Two: Stop the Hurt
  This section is a cluster of chapters (7-14) describing various techniques and tools that can overcome self-defeating traps that bullied Targets can fall into. Most of the chapters have practical exercises to guide individuals from the negative to the positive. It is the toolkit part of the book, the heart of BullyProofing yourself.

- ## Section Three: Moving On, Up or Out
  First, we give a brief overview of The Work Doctor's approach to BullyBusting, with a little help from friends. It is an elaborate process that is rarely successful because of the vast resources organized against the individual employee. We hate to give bad, but realistic, news. Finally, we address the question of leaving a job when personal sacrifices are unreasonably high.

If you have a spouse or life-partner who also shares the experience, the journey out of Targethood must be taken by you both. Therefore, it is a good idea to have that person and caring acquaintances become familiar with the first section of the book, to be able to share the terminology and to appreciate the seriousness of your situation.

You Are Not Alone!

Disclaimer

Dear Reader:

This book contains information, suggestions and opinions about improving the quality of people's lives from the authors. The use, misuse, understanding or misunderstanding of the material, in whole or part, is the sole responsibility of the reader.

Neither the publisher nor authors assume responsibility or liability, jointly or individually to any person, group, organization or entity regarding any emotional or material loss, damage or injury caused or alleged to be caused directly or indirectly by the information contained in this book.

Readers experiencing negative emotional reactions to the material are advised to seek professional counseling. Readers for whom the information proves liberating, exhilirating or empowering are invited to tell everyone they know.

If you do not wish to be bound by the above, you may return this book to the publisher for a full refund.

Gary and Ruth Namie

The Campaign Against Workplace Bullying
P.O. Box 1886
Benicia, CA 94510

707-747-9000
707-745-6630
888-FIX-WORK

Section One

The Silent Epidemic Exposed

In Memory of Heinz Leymann

Chapter 1
Bullying At Work

In the societies of the highly industrialized western world, the workplace is the only remaining battlefield where people can "kill" each other without running the risk of being taken to court.   - Heinz Leymann, M.D.

Our Definition

Bullying is the **deliberate, hurtful** and **repeated** mistreatment of a Target (the recipient) by a bully (the perpetrator) that is driven by the bully's **desire to control** the Target.

Bullying is harassment. Bullying encompasses all types of mistreatment at work. All harassment is bullying as long as the actions have the effect, intended or not, of hurting the Target, if felt by the Target.

Bullying Is Different

Incivilities and rudeness rarely trigger stress in the people who experience them. Toe picking, knuckle cracking, belching and nostril reaming are all offensive and undignified. However, they reflect only on the socialization of the picker, cracker, belcher and reamer. It's not bullying until the bully does something to the Target. If the bully picks the Target's toes (against her wishes) or picks her nose (without permission) and this offensive behavior hurts her emotionally, it could be bullying. Inadvertent social mistakes not expressly done to affect another person may be cute to talk about, but they do not qualify as bullying according to our criteria.

Illegal sexual harassment is a special type of harassment. All sexual harassment is also bullying.

Bullying is **rarely illegal**. Either the law does not apply or the way to build a case is too difficult for average attorneys to discover. Harassment unrelated to gender or race or age or any of the other Title VII (of the Civil Rights Act) protected classes leaves the Target mostly unprotected by current law.

"Protection" is a misnomer. Laws on the books are routinely ignored in the American workplace anyway. Sexual harassment and the hostile work environment are pervasive. The hostility continues despite millions of dollars invested in corporate training claiming to prevent or stop it.

We all know that employees smirk at each management fad shoved down their throats. Without swift, public punishment of violators, training becomes laughable. We've all seen the eye-rolling and exchange of "and-this-too-shall-pass" looks.

The presence of a law simply gives one the "right to sue." In turn, that means placing yourself in financial jeopardy at the hands of a befuddled attorney, pro-corporate judge or jury whose decisions can be easily overruled over the course of several years. Even when the settlement or award is paid, the payoff hardly justifies prolonging the agony that bullying started. Legal solutions are rarely satisfying.

We use the term workplace bullying to refer to the mistreatment that afflicts at least 1 in 4 workers, according to a 1993 survey conducted by Northwestern National Life Insurance company. It is that unconscionable mistreatment which can devastate an employee's life, career and family.

Schoolyard bullying—the torment of one child by another— is often compared to workplace bullying. Both types share common underlying principles—the desperate grab for control, the exercise of power and the role of humiliation to shame the Target. However, the stakes for workplace bullying affect the economic livelihood not only of the Target but the Target's family. When a bully decides to capriciously untrack a Target's career, years of investment in terms of time and money, are at risk. Finally, the most important difference, the one that distinguishes our approach to solutions, is that the child Target *must* have the help and support of third-party adults to reverse the conflict. Bullied adults have the primary responsibility for righting the wrong, for engineering a solution. When others intervene on their behalf—as when a more aggressive, well-intentioned spouse takes over finding the solution—the Targets suffer additional consequences from deferring their independence.

In all harassment and bullying cases, our goal is to have the Target reclaim as much of the stolen self-respect and dignity she can, as quickly as she can.

International Roots of the Anti-Bullying Movement

The late Heinz Leymann, the Swedish pioneer, treated victims of workplace "mobbing," in his clinic. He holds the equivalent of two doctorates (M.D. and Ph.D.) which enabled him to not only work to heal victims but to conduct research at the same time. His scientific publications on the topic began in the 1980's. Here is his definition of mobbing, his term for workplace bullying.

> "Psychological terror or mobbing in working life involves hostile and unethical communication which is directed in a systematic manner by one or more individuals, mainly toward one individual, who, due to mobbing, is pushed into a helpless and defenseless position and held there by means of continuing mobbing activities. These actions occur on a very frequent basis (statistical definition: at least once a week) and over a long period of time (statistical definition: at least six months' duration). Because of the high frequency and long duration of hostile behavior, this maltreatment results in considerable mental, psychosomatic and social misery."

Note that Dr. Leymann focuses on the impact on the Target. He writes that the level of PTSD (post-traumatic stress) suffered by mobbing victims is more intense and persistent than that felt by train operators who witnessed suicides by people leaping onto railroad tracks in front of them.

Leymann's concern is the set of medical stress consequences of bullying for the Target rather than with classifying personal types or re-engineering organizations. We, too, have made helping Targets our first priority.

Leymann also claims that the chances of healing from an acute (and normal) trauma from bullying are reduced if the individual faces continuing threats. As long as the perpetrator goes unpunished, or the victim does not receive effective support, he or she can be torn to pieces again at any time.

The trauma is sustained by loss of income, spouses running from the discomfort, EAP counselors, the personnel department, insensitive (or disbelieving) managers, co-workers, union reps, doctors in general practice, the company's insurance carrier, state disability agencies, and lawyers and the courts, if legal steps are pursued.

In the United Kingdom

British journalist Andrea Adams coined the phrase "workplace bullying" based on her 1988 investigation of the mistreatment of employees in a bank. She reported on bullying for BBC radio and wrote the first book in the United Kingdom on how to confront and overcome bullying in 1992. Tragically, she lost her personal battle with cancer in November, 1995.

In the UK, unions have assumed the mantle of leadership. It is they who provide national awareness campaigns, telephone hotlines to report mistreating employers and support. There are several individual pioneers and crusaders who also contribute much to the public movement—Andrew Ellis (who administers a national bullying bulletin board on the internet), Tim Field (author, founder of the UK bullying hotline and web site host) and Vicki Merchant (founder of the International Harassment Network).

Workers in the UK have the opportunity to complain about their employers in Employment (formerly Industrial) Tribunals.

Academic researchers in the UK, like Charlotte Rayner of the Staffordshire University Business School and the Andrea Adams Trust, work collaboratively with unions to design and analyze workplace surveys. One such independent study was conducted by UNISON, a union representing workers in public service organizations.

According to the 1996 UNISON survey:

- 66% of the respondents either experienced or witnessed workplace bullying.

- Of those being repeatedly bullied, 74% said management knew about it.

- A whopping 94% thought the bullies could get away with it.

- 83% of bullies were managers.

- Over 75% of the bullied reported some damage to their health—stress, depression and lowered self-confidence were the most common psychological complaints.

In Australia

In 1994, four Australians—two business school professors, a psychiatrist and a school psychologist—convened their country's first conference on bullying. The four founders of the Beyond Bullying Association had concluded that bullying was a major problem in the schools, homes and workplaces. The BBA works to create codes of conduct for schools, prisons and workplaces and to develop guidelines for laws protecting individuals from harassment.

EuroLaws About Bullying

Bullying at work is increasingly seen as an important issue throughout Europe. Scandinavian countries in particular have recognized bullying as a work environment or health and safety issue and have introduced measures to prevent it.

For example, Norway recently improved its Work Environment Act to provide protection to employees against bullying at work.

In Sweden, an ordinance on measures against victimization at work came into force in March, 1994. This defines victimization as *"recurrent reprehensible or distinctly negative actions which are directed against individual employees in an of-*

fensive manner and can result in those employees being placed outside the workplace community."

The ordinance makes clear that this includes adult bullying, mental violence, social rejection, harassment and offensive administrative sanctions. The ordinance requires employers to:

- Plan and organize work so as to prevent victimization.

- Make clear that victimization cannot be accepted.

- Provide routines for the early detection of, signs of, and the elimination of, such unsatisfactory working conditions, problems of work organization or deficiencies of co-operation as can provide a basis for victimization.

- Implement countermeasures without delay if signs of victimization become apparent, including investigation of whether the way in which work is organized may be a cause.

- Have special routines to provide rapid help and support to employees who are subjected to victimization.

The Swedish legislation makes it clear that bullying is an organizational issue and that employers have a duty to organize work and the work environment, so that it does not provide the sort of climate in which bullying is likely to occur.

Laws in the United Kingdom indirectly prohibiting bullying invoke either Health and Safety or Employment Law codes.

Employers have general duties to protect employees' health and to consult safety representatives about health and safety matters. Furthermore, every employer has a legal duty to make a suitable and sufficient assessment of the risks to the health and safety of their employees while they are at work.

Although not explicitly stated, the employer's duty to protect employees' health should be taken as referring to both physical **and mental health** and the employer should assess the risks to both.

The British Health and Safety Executive (HSE) has published guidance for employers on preventing stress at work which makes it clear that **bullying can be a cause of stress** and that preventive measures must include action to eliminate bullying where it exists.

According to UK tort law, employers also have a general **duty of care** for their employees. It allows the victim to claim damages where the victim suffers some injury.

In certain circumstances, where bullying leads to a fundamental breach of the employment contract and is serious enough for the employee to terminate without notice, an employee may be able to pursue a claim of constructive dismissal. Contractual terms can be expressed in written form, as in a labor agreement, or implied. Typical examples of implied contract terms would be "mutual trust and confidence" or the statutory term to "provide a safe system of work." Employees can take their claims to Employment Tribunals.

Sometimes the English judiciary can be far reaching and imaginative when it comes to interpreting a statute. For instance, if an individual manager or a company is found responsible for causing psychological harm (a recognized psychiatric illness like PTSD, for instance) the mistreatment may constitute either Actual Bodily Harm (a violation of the Offences Against the Persons Act, punishable by up to 5 years imprisonment) or Grievous Bodily Harm if committed with intent. The latter offense qualifies the perpetrator for a life sentence, a sentence rarely imposed.

America Takes Its First Steps

The U.S. is at least 18 years behind Sweden, 10 years behind England and four behind Australia on focusing on workplace conduct. Thanks to the media obsession with the mantras—'globalization,' 'competitiveness,' and 'productivity'— our attention gets diverted from the mistreatment of colleagues at work. We are bamboozled into mistaking the Dow Jones average for an index of the national mood, while ignoring completely personal accomplishments that feed our souls rather than the pocketbook.

Let's recruit competition to do some good. We had better catch up with the rest of the world to stop bullying as a demonstration of America's parallel leadership in the arenas of economic dominance and compassion for those who do the work!

> *Whenever you are in doubt...apply the first test. Recall the face of the poorest and the weakest man whom you may have seen, and ask yourself if the step you contemplate is going to be any use to him. Will he gain anything from it? Will it restore him to a control over his own life and destiny? True development puts first those that society puts last.*
> *- Mahatma Gandhi*

Loraleigh Keashly, a professor of Urban and Labor Studies at Wayne State University in Detroit, reviewed the work done in the American academic community on bullying-related topics. Her 1998 report describes how the more socially acceptable forms of emotional abuse in the workplace are beginning to be studied. However, physical violence and sexual-racial harassment still generate the most interest.

The frequency of studies increased in the 1990's though some date back to 1986. They called this "socially acceptable" form of primarily verbal violence "incivilities," "intolerable behavior," "interpersonal sources of job stress," and "workplace aggression."

It was Keashly herself who chose the label "emotional abuse" in the workplace. She defines it as the hostile verbal and nonverbal behaviors, independent of racial or sexual content, directed at a person to gain control over, even subservience from, that person.

Keashly's Dimensions of Emotional Abuse (EA)
1. EA can include verbal and physical expressions
2. Pattern of repeated behaviors
3. EA behaviors are unwelcome, unwanted, unsolicited
4. EA violates standards of humane treatment, moral obligation, ethics
5. EA behaviors cause harm
6. There is intent or an ability to control
7. Power differences

The work of Joel Neuman, a management professor at the State University of New York at New Paltz, explores organizational conditions related to the frequency of workplace aggression and factors, both personal and workplace-related, that predict a bully's hostility. Many of his studies of aggression point to the increasing rate and extent of change facing employees and managers. His work bridges the gap between macro-economics and impact on individual lives.

Another noteworthy professor, David Yamada, at Suffolk University Law School in Boston, deserves praise. His body of work reflects a commitment to applying the law to labor and the less advantaged. He currently is investigating ways that the law can be used to serve the needs of bullied Targets. Too often, lazy unmotivated lawyers reject cases that bullied Targets bring to them because the law does not provide explicit protections. But the fight for justice in the current system can be won. Less direct interpretations of existing, albeit limited, laws by clever, motivated attorneys can win justice for Targets. Soon, Yamada hopes to draft statutes that states can adopt to give lawyers the weaponry to combat harassing, destructive bullies at work.

Except for a sprinkling of independent thinkers like Keashly, Neuman and Yamada, most academicians do not wish to risk angering their university employers, government and foundation underwriters, or corporate executives at whose right hand most professors long to serve as highly paid consultants. To conduct research about the dysfunctional American workplace is to appear to challenge the popular alliance between universities and business.

The public does not expect academic researchers to lead America in the crusade against workplace bullying, but they have the chance to contribute knowledge to those afflicted in two ways. First, the studies have to be meaningful to working people, to ask questions about important matters at work, not trivia. Surveying college freshmen does no good. Neither does conducting workplace studies under the watchful gaze of paranoid executives looking for a way to squeeze more work out of employees who find themselves doing more with fewer co-workers to share the load. Second, findings must be communicated to workers in non-academic jargon through channels that employees can readily access.

The Campaign Against Workplace Bullying (CAWB)

It was unofficially launched on January 1, 1998 on the internet at The Work Doctor's original web site (**www.workdoctor.com**). The Campaign now has itw own home on the internet at **www.bullybusters.org**.

Ruth and Gary Namie converted their growing advice and counseling service for employees into a new national nonprofit organization in late 1998. Ruth is the psychotherapist, with a doctorate in clinical psychology; Gary is the social/organizational psychologist, 'recovering academic' and 'reformed management consultant.' Since 1996, we have advised thousands of people via e-mail and telephone. The vicarious experiences of others and Ruth's personal battle with a first-class bully led us to start the Campaign. Gary does facts; Ruth does feelings.

The Campaign, through its directors, advisory board and outreach to affiliated individuals and other organizations, leads the fight against workplace bullying. Headquarters are in the San Francisco Bay Area.

The Campaign prefers the term "bullying" so as to not infringe on the rights of youngsters and vulnerable victims by using the term "abuse." Though we are psychologists, we know that no one would be caught dead in public saying "interpersonal antecedents of reciprocated, cue-driven aggression." When people say "bullying," it seems to be instantly understood. It simplifies the awareness-raising effort.

There is no confusion with childhood bullying when adults are talking about the torment they face in the workplace. They automatically know that this is serious talk about important matters. The Campaign credits our British predecessors for the term's instant credibility.

The Campaign exists to serve Targets, current, future and past. Its constituency is similar to Leymann's and the UK unions.

The mission of the grassroots Campaign is twofold:

(1) to raise public awareness (of bullying) and initiate a national dialogue, and

(2) to create and promote solutions for individuals and workplaces.

There are three strategic areas for the Campaign to tackle in the years ahead. Here they are, ranked from immediate to future priority.

- Education, Support & Advice for Individuals (Targets)
- workshops, speeches for interested groups of any size
- a national toll-free call center for advice and support
- coordinating a national grassroots network of Field Advocates, local support groups, and peer counselors
- counseling for individuals & couples about bullying's impact
- training for professionals with the opportunity to help bullied Targets
- expert witness and advocacy services in the legal and dispute resolution arena
- publications: books, educational materials
- coordination and staging of national, regional and local conventions for Targets; participation in related conferences designed by other organizations
- translating and disseminating the relevant work of U.S. academic and legal researchers
- polling bullied Targets and disseminating results

- Alliances with groups that promote employees' rights and fight workplace harassment
- Women's rights organizations, unions, management associations, government workers, plaintiffs-only attorney groups

- System changes—for employers, for legislators who now are not willing to lower the threshold for making general forms of harassment illegal.

The Campaign Survey Says

On Labor Day 1998, the Campaign released results from the first 200 surveys completed online at the web site by Targets and witnesses of workplace bullying. In all, 154 Targets and 46 Witnesses completed surveys. Sixty-six Targets also completed a questionnaire about the aftermath of the bullying situation.

Though the sample of respondents does not represent a randomly representative group, thus rendering the study a "non-scientific" one, it is a look directly into the belly of the beast which too many of our sick workplaces represent.

The rationale for the surveys was to document the breadth and depth of the bullying phenomenon as reported by those closest to it for those who may experience it either as recipients or witnesses in the future. We hope the indisputable facts will somehow soften the blow for Targets and shorten their recovery time.

Major Survey Findings

1) <u>Bullying is different</u> from the more recognizable issues that plague the workplace — sexual harassment, racial discrimination and violence. Both women and men are victimized as Targets and serve as perpetrators.

2) Falling prey to a bully's destructive tactics is <u>a career hazard</u>; it is not about gamesmanship or a fair competition among equals. Bullies commonly adopt surprise and secrecy to gain leverage over Targets.

3) <u>Targets are a diverse group</u> of normal, talented people.

4) <u>Bullying devastates</u> the Target's emotional stability and <u>can last a long time.</u>

5) The <u>employer, as an organization, bears partial responsibility</u> for the systematic disassembly of a once productive employee by a mean-spirited one-person wrecking crew.

Whenever a survey finding is relevant to the topic under discussion, you'll find a special Campaign Survey Says box.

American Law: Missing in Action

The law is attentive to harassment or discrimination when it relates to sex and race. Title VII of the 1964 (revised in 1991) Civil Rights Act created "protected classes" of individuals. Members of protected classes have a lower burden of proof than members of other groups when harassment or discrimination is claimed.

Many ostensibly "disadvantaged" individuals who harass others consider themselves immune to punishment for their deeds. Protected class members are often the worst bullies. Too often, they threaten lawsuits, based on race or gender, to scare away co-workers and employers who want them to stop harassing. The classic formula is for a woman or minority bully to shout discrimination as Targets begin countermeasures. Organizations then settle for cash with the bully, allowing her to stay on the job and force the Target to leave. The message is sent that the bully has the full backing of the organization, gets cash for bullying and has the full force of U.S. federal law behind her.

There is little reason for optimism that federal prohibition of general harassment is forthcoming. In fact, in the 1998 season of rulings by the U.S. Supreme Court, there were three rulings that we consider relevant.

In late June, the Court ruled on two cases putting employers on notice that they can be held responsible for misconduct by supervisors even if they knew nothing about it.

The Court said employees have to first "take advantage of any preventive or corrective opportunities provided." This is exactly what we tell those who seek our advice about bullying,

exhaust the often silly internal procedures to cover your behind. The worst thing a Target can do is to keep secret all that
she is going through.

The good news is that a threat, whether acted on or not,
such as, "You know, Kim, I could make your life very hard or
very easy at Burlington" was sufficient to create a hostile environment for which the unknowing employer was liable. In the
second case involving a Florida city lifeguard, the city was liable for two supervisors' inappropriate touching & comments
because it had no complaint procedures.

The implications from the late June, 1998 decisions are good
for enemies of bullying. More credence is now being given to
"hostile environment" cases. Much of the repeated mistreatment that characterizes bullying relies on a poisoned, sick workplace to permit and sustain the madness.

The Campaign Survey Says . . .

✓ In 89% of the cases, bullies were the Target's bosses

✓ To Targets, the *least* helpful groups were Human
   Resources (3% helped) and Senior Management
   (7.6%) vs. support from Co-Workers (95% or 72%,
   depending if you asked the co-workers or Targets)

However, most important was the Supreme Court's March
1998 decision. It dimmed hope that harassment's definition will
ever be broadened in the eyes of the law.

Justice Antonin Scalia, writing for the unanimous Court,
explicitly stated the law "does not prohibit all verbal or physical harassment in the workplace ... And there is another re-
quirement that *prevents* (our emphasis) Title VII from expand-

ing into a general civility code ... the statute does not reach genuine but innocuous differences in the ways men and women routinely interact...

Common sense and an appropriate sensitivity to social context will enable courts and juries to distinguish between simple teasing or roughhousing ... and conduct which a reasonable person in the plaintiff's position would find severely hostile or abusive."

This means the Court turned away from using discrimination law to enforce a general code of civility banning all workplace harassment. Looking from the top down, rather than through the eyes of a bullied Target, much harassment looks "innocuous," to be mere personality conflicts.

Reactions to the Court Rulings

A *Washington Post* newspaper editorial reaction to the Court's ruling saw the coupling of harassment to discrimination as missing the point. The *Post* called for Congress to write specific anti-harassment laws that do not require sex, race or national origin protections, but instead require only that a work environment be sufficiently abusive. The editorial stated, "what bothers people about abusive workplace conduct, after all, is not the fact that it may be discriminatory but that it is abusive in the first place."

Employers see themselves as the "reasonable person" who can then define a harasser's conduct as hostile rather than the simple teasing of a Target who needs to have a thicker skin. Stephen Bokat, spokesman for the National Chamber Litigation Center, the business defense arm for the U.S. Chamber of Commerce, believed the ruling would actually make it easier for employers to defend themselves. He felt that more complaints will be dismissed as boisterous horseplay or casual flirting. See— it's just your imagination.

Bokat trivialized workplace harassment and discrimination problems with a glib comment to the Associated Press, "I don't think it happens that often."

And we are sure he does not acknowledge that women harass other women in such a see/hear/say/do-nothing world of employers in denial.

The Campaign Survey Says . . .

✓ **Women** Targets were bullied by **women**
    in 46% of the cases
✓ Men Targets were bullied by women
    in only 28% of the cases
✓ EEOC-complaint criteria (race or gender
        discrimination) applied in under 10%
        of the situations
Bullying is different than Title VII harassment

A Call to Action

Do not wait for leaders; do it alone, person to person.
- Mother Teresa

It is an uphill fight to be sure. In our media-saturated world, messages for and about regular workers are rare. One former business reporter was so frustrated by the fawning over CEOs, investors, entrepreneurs, and consumers that he started an online magazine www.disgruntled.com. There, he is able to tell stories from the employee's point of view. Daniel Levine is one of those rare advocates for employees. His 1998 book, *Disgruntled: The Darker Side of the World of Work*, speaks with a candor rarely seen in the mainstream press or heard in broadcasts. We join *Disgruntled* in the fight.

Because U.S. politicians are currently more inclined to reverse physical safety protections in the workplace rather than to augment them with psychological safety guidelines and the Supreme Court will not judicially lower the bar for harassment, our initial and ongoing attention must be given to individuals torn to shreds daily by bullies with the tacit approval of employers and the general public. But we have one eye on changing organizations that further harass bullied workers via impossible internal procedures that pretend to investigate bullies. And our third eye is on contributing to changes in the law to begin to level the playing field for people who work for a living.

Silence and shame ensure that bullying will never stop. We must work to uncover and reverse the atrocities, one person, one company and one law at a time.

Chapter 2
The Target—Bully Tango

There is exploitation when an owner consid-
ers workers not as his associates or auxiliaries
but as instruments from whom to obtain the
most service at the least possible cost. The ex-
ploitation of man by man is slavery.
-Antoine Frederic Ozanam
19th century co-founder of
St. Vincent de Paul Societies

It normally takes two to make a relationship grow from an initial spark. This is true for love and for some exploitative relationships, too. In most couples, each person wants something. Otherwise nothing develops. Ideally, a partnership blooms with interwoven dependencies.

On the other hand, the Target-Bully "relationship" is different because:

- the bully and only the bully starts it

- mutual benefit or gain is not the goal, control is, and the Target wants none of it

- the undermining, scheming bully's tactics are so unwelcome, inappropriate and undeserved that in no way can the Target be held responsible, even partially responsible

- it is impossible to rationalize that the slave (as Ozanam puts it) benefits from exploitation

- bullies need Targets to live; Targets find it hard to live when bullies intrude in their lives

> *The people have always some champion whom they*
> *set over them and nurse into greatness ... This and*
> *no other is the root from which a tyrant springs.*
> *- Plato*

Let's take a brief look bullies so you can recognize them based on the games they play that threaten the careers, families and lives of Targets. First we explore what gets bullies started. Then, we'll categorize bullies into four simple (but not exhaustive) groups.

After covering bullies, we look at characteristics of Targets likely to attract bullies. Finally, we list some symptoms of sick workplaces that encourage and sustain bullying.

Bully Origins

Bullies follow different paths to bullyhood. We define three breeding grounds for bullies: the tyrant's personality, the political workplace, and accidental trip-ups.

The Chronic Bully

The Chronic bully is the classic, stereotypical bully that everyone thinks of. She probably was a brash, pushy kid at school and kept pushing people around as an adult. Since most people are afraid of someone like this, she's used to getting her way. It's a self-reinforcing cycle. She dominates, others submit, so she dominates more.

The Chronic bully is also the most consistent across time and place. She is the most frequent abuser of others at work. In hard-driving companies, (since they are great competitors), she is over-represented among the ranks of the "climbers." She bullies waitresses at restaurants as well as new employees (to test their willingness to allow her to control) at work. She will be the type to say "I can't help it. It's just who I am. Don't like it? Leave" always believing that she neither can nor has to change.

Some Chronic bullies are trapped by their personality, they couldn't change even if they wanted to (and most don't!). It could be traced to the learning of bad habits (the reinforcement cycle) instead of genetics. It is true that some Chronic bullies have genuinely certifiable mental disorders —either an Antisocial or Narcissistic Personality Disorder. But just having a personality disorder or an awareness of it doesn't excuse them. In the general population, these types of people are statistically rare, hovering around 2-3%.

Targets should know that simply being able to identify the bully by psychopathological characteristics does not change the situation. Too much psychobabble will get you classified as the nut.

Bullies Are Inadequate, Defective & Poorly Developed People Targets Are Empathic, Fair People Deserving Justice

The chronic bully is the most dangerous bully because they are the most practiced at the art of destroying others. They are actually malevolent, mean-spirited and downright nasty. They manipulate everyone on some level. They inflict harm on others. Chronic bullies end careers and shatter the emotional lives of their targets.

As a Target, you need to be less concerned with <u>why</u> bullies do what they do as with <u>how to stop the hurt</u> from their actions.

It is safe to say that the underlying motivation of the Chronic bully is her own sense of inadequacy. It is so great that everything she does is calculated (automatically after a lifetime of practice) to hide that self-loathing. Some colleagues suggest forgiveness for the harm done.

We take our lead from veteran Targets who several years later regret not confronting the bully, and being chased away from the situation without once declaring their outrage over the unilateral harassment endured.

The Opportunistic Bully

The Opportunistic bully is the one you're more likely to encounter at work. She is master at reading cues from the workplace. If competition is expected, she knows that beating up other people will be tolerated in a culture caught up in winning. Only "wimps" would stand in a competitor's path and have her slow down to pay attention to how people might be injured.

She's the normal woman away from work—capable of being friendly, charming, supportive, she might even host a youth group meeting in her home, She's a great mother, churchgoer, neighborhood activist, blah, blah.

However, at work, when the opportunity presents itself to compete and obliterate a co-worker (the Target), she seizes the chance, always hustling. Though companies preach cooperation and teamwork, look at what is actually rewarded. The Opportunistic bully recognizes this and never wants to be a "chump." To be a chump is to be a loser; she never loses.

The Opportunistic bully loves competition and prizes her keen ability to anticipate chances to move ahead. As part of the struggle, others may get hurt, but she would say "that's all part of the game." Understand that games, to this bully, are serious business. Career building is based on gamesmanship, according to her mindset. Can you see that the corporate mentality is the same as hers?

When companies lay-off 10,000 employees to maintain their profit margins to satisfy Wall Street—a deliberate act of malice—how do they justify it? "It's just business, nothing personal." Those moments of seizing market opportunities without regard to consequences for humans makes organizations themselves Opportunistic bullies.

The Opportunistic bully has learned well the lessons of the contemporary workplace and is likely to be well connected up the chain of command. She has allies above to shield her from punishment for her malicious behavior. However, it is not in her blood, except when she comes to work.

Of course, she is fooling herself to believe that she can preserve a solid boundary between work and the rest of her life. Over time, the line gets blurred. Unscrupulous, competitive behavior starts to trickle into every aspect of her life. When leading a church fundraiser, she sets the goal too high, just to keep everyone striving harder than they should. Little lies creep into her marriage, but she figures that she will be excused because circumstances made her do it.

Ultimately, the Opportunistic bully has trouble accepting personal responsibility for anything, because she was simply responding to situations that others created for her. Since this style is so much a part of American mass culture, she is not seen as a bad person except by the Target she hurts on her quest for personal success. Targets have a hard time convincing senior management that she has done anything wrong. This bully is the personification of "the American dream."

The Accidental Bully

This is the rarest of the three types of workplace bullies. She is simply, and forgivably, a social fool. The Accidental bully is truly *unaware* of the effect of her actions on other people.

You have seen people like this. They operate as if the rest of the world does not exist. They are awkward, in a child-like way. There is an innocence about them, with the downside being that they can hurt.

The hurt comes from inappropriate comments or actions. They will say sexist things. They will state that you are incompetent. They will start to show you how to do something, then do the job themselves because they do not have the patience to wait for you to learn something new.

There is a subtle difference in body language and nonverbal communication style, that also sets the Accidental bully apart from the others.

The others have an ability to drill through you with their intensity. The Accidental bully is not intent on hurting, therefore, she lacks the intensity or competitive zeal. She just never learned the subtlety of positive social interaction.

The test to tell whether the person is an Accidental bully or one of the other two types is to immediately confront her when the hurtful remark or action happens.

Only the Accidental bully will apologize, obviously embarrassed at having her social ineptitude revealed. Others would get defensive and counterattack or escalate the hostility.

The remarkable thing about Accidental bullies is that when confronted, they retreat immediately and apologize and they never do the same thing to you again. They are not stupid. They *can* learn the social skill you just taught them.

To the Accidental bully, most companies are threatening places. They risk making social errors. Some companies have tasks that require no interaction; this type of bully does well there (do we see pocket protectors?). The Accidental bully does best by working in a home office (though risking social errors on the telephone) or by telecommuting.

Bullies: Types & Tactics

Bullies are workplace politicians. Their goal is simple—to control people they target. To do this, they engage in a variety of tactics. Regardless of tactics adopted, they all serve to shame, humiliate and treat the Target like a powerless person. In their minds, Targets are powerless. This distorted thinking is the only way bullies know how to survive the workworld, at someone else's expense.

> ## Bullies Start All Conflict & Trouble
> ## Targets React, They Don't Start It

Bullies can be categorized, as is done in this section. But individuals who choose to bully can adopt any tactic at any time to accomplish their goal. They are not restricted to neat categories. They adopt one or more styles, as needed.

A short list of illustrative tactics accompanies each type of bully. The list is not meant to be exhaustive. You can probably think of many more tricks each type plays.

Constant Critic

Extremely negative. Nitpicker. Perfectionist. Whiner. Complainer. Fault finder. Lies. Masks personal insecurity with public bravado. Loved by senior management because of her ability to "get those people to produce." Plays Parent to your Child (as she sees it). Aims to destroy confidence, encourages self-doubt.

- put-downs, insults, belittling comments, name-calling

- constant haranguing about Target's "incompetence"

- makes aggressive eye contact, glaring at the Target; demands eye contact when she speaks but deliberately avoids eye contact when Target speaks

- negatively reacts to Target contributions with sighs, frowns, peering over top of eyeglasses to condescend, sour face (the "just sucked a lemon" look)

- accuses Target of wrongdoing, blamed for errors made up by bully (doctored documents, compromised databases, fake witness accounts)

- makes unreasonable demands for work with impossible deadlines, applies disproportionate pressure, expects perfectionism

- sends signals of disrespect through hyper-confident body language—sitting at desk with feet up, showing target bottom of shoes and talking to target through feet, bully grooms self (hair, nails) while ignoring the Target; making target sit while bully stands, hovering over, staying above

- overuses memos, e-mails, messages to bury Target in correspondence requiring replies

- personally criticizes aspects of the Target's life that are irrelevant to work—appearance, family, friends

- excessively or harshly criticizes Target's work or abilities

- engages Target in intense cross-examination to belittle and confuse

Two—Headed Snake

Passive-Aggressive indirect, dishonest style of dealing with people and issues. Jekyll-Hyde. Pretends to be nice while sabotaging you. "Friendliness" serves only to decrease resistance to giving information she may later use against you. Smile hides naked aggression. Assassinates reputation with higher ups. Plays favorites.

- ensures that the Target does not have the resources (time, supplies, help) to do work

- demands that co-workers provide damning "evidence" against Target, uses lies or half-truths, threatens non-cooperators (the "divide and conquer" technique)

- discriminates against smokers by requiring they gather trash from the parking lot while taking a smoke break

- assigns meaningless or "dirty" tasks as punishment

- makes nasty, rude, hostile remarks directly to Target while putting on a rational "face" for others

- breaches confidentiality; shares private information about the Target with co-workers or other bosses

- discriminates against non-smoking Target by permitting breaks only for smokers

- creates a special personnel file kept in bully's car or locked in her office full of defamatory information to sabotage Target's career inside or outside the organization

- steals credit for work done by the Target

Gatekeeper

Most transparent of the controllers. She needs to establish herself as "one up" on you, to order you around or to control your circumstances. To her, control of all resources (time, supplies, praise, approval, money, staffing, help) is the most important aspect of work. Approval must be solicited from her.

- deliberately cuts the Target out of the communication loop—stops mail, e-mail, memo distribution, doesn't return calls

- refuses to make "reasonable accommodation" for a Target returning to work with a disability

- refuses to follow internal policies and government-mandated employee protections for Target

- denies privileges and rights to Targets who file complaints against the bully, either an internal complaint or a lawsuit or with the EEOC, DOL

- ignores the Target; gives the "silent treatment," and models isolation/exclusion for others

- sets office clocks 15 minutes ahead of "real" time, then punishes Target for being "late" at start of day, while not allowing her to leave before quitting time according to "real" time

- makes up new rules on a whim, Target expected to follow, but bully is exempt

Screaming Mimi

Stereotypical bully. Controls through fear & intimidation. Emotionally out of control. Impulsive. Volatile. Explosive. Threat of physical violence becomes issue. Wants to instill sense of dread. Overbearing. Self-centered, insensitive to needs of others. Very worried about being detected as imposter. Bombast masks incompetence.

- yells, screams, curses

- barks out loud often that "I AM THE BOSS!!!!" "DO WHAT I TELL YOU!!!"

- poisons workplace with angry outbursts, tantrums

- intimidates through gestures: finger pointing, slams things down, throws objects

- crowds the Target's personal space, moves close to threaten or to make the Target anxious, hovers over, sneaks up from behind to startle

- constantly interrupts the Target during meetings and conversations

- discounts and denies Target's thoughts or feelings

- threatens job loss or punitive transfer

- traps Target by insisting that complaints go "up the chain of command," starting with her

The Campaign Survey Says . . .

Top Ten Bullying Tactics
1 Blame for "errors"
2 Unreasonable job demands
3 Criticism of ability
4 Inconsistent compliance with rules
5 Threatens job loss
6 Insults and put-downs
7 Discounting/denial of accomplishments
8 Exclusion, "icing out"
9 Yelling, screaming
10 Stealing credit

Target Types

Bullies don't usually torment everyone. The factors that affect a bully's Target selection criteria include: the depth of the bully's inadequacy, her own transient self-esteem at that given moment, position at work, ability to bully without being punished, the Target's resistance, the amount of road rage siphoned off during the morning commute, time in the lunar calendar and the Target's personality.

The Campaign Survey Says . . .

Targets are Everywoman, Everyman
- ✓ 29.5% of Targets held a graduate or professional degree; 27.5% had a 4 yr. college degree
- ✓ 78% of those surveyed were 24 - 46 years old
- ✓ Employers were divided among private sector (59.3%), 25.3% in government, and 15.4% nonprofit firms

Targets share at least one common trait—a tendency to cooperate. This will be explained more in Chapter 4. However, it is interesting to note that bullied Targets come in at least three types, one or two of which may surprise you.

Nice People

Bullies eat "nice" people alive. Bullies are competitors and live for the opportunity to work with a bunch of cooperators. Imagine the glee of a sadistic supervisor who inherits a group of positive, but non-combative people to manage.

In light of all the talk about "team-ness" being central to successful work performance in most contemporary American workplaces, it is ironic that the people with a more advanced stage of human development (the ability to cooperate) fall prey to the primitive, neanderthal bullies.

Research shows that when everyone cooperates, groups maximize benefits to each person. They get more goodies, whatever goodies there are. But the human tendency to grab the most for oneself prevails in studies with groups that have chances to build a collective cash pool. The rules typically call for a doubling of the amount of cash in a bowl if no one person withdraws money from the bowl during a round of a game.

Unfortunately, groups break the bank and rarely play more than one round. This happens because greedy individuals (from a random group of people sitting around the table) snatch the money bowl for themselves, ruining the game for others. They do this despite being free to talk out loud, to formulate a strategy, to agree to keep doubling money that could be split later.

The reality of the workplace is no different. The formal, written rules call for teamwork, dangling the biggest prizes to groups that cooperate. Operating rules, however, undermine cooperation. Bullies, as strong competitors, know that if they grab "goodies" at the expense of Targets, they win. The cooperators are left to watch the competitor dictate the outcomes (gains or losses) they will experience.

It is clear in the competitive workplace populated with bullies, cooperators are second-class citizens. Americans hate being second. In the face of a winner-take-all world, cooperators don't stand a chance without a concerted institutional effort to wrest control of the rules away from greedy bullies.

Cooperators are not weak; they are simply over-optimistic that goodwill will naturally and automatically prevail. Bullies interpret "nice" as the unlikeliness to confront or stop them.

Vulnerable People

Bullies scan groups for the weakest. Maybe it is an evolutionary remnant of our place in the animal kingdom. All predatory species select and attack the weakest prey. It's done for food. Barely human bullies only symbolically eat their prey. Their sustenance is the fear they instill in Targets.

Many Targets look and sound like a non-threatening person to the bully. This is done with both words and nonverbal messages communicated to the bully.

Vulnerability Through Words

Self-effacing statements can be a sign of humility or civility. In those instances, we hear lots of praise heaped on others, a genuine desire to deflect credit that she herself deserves. "I could not have done this alone. There are many others to thank." "My co-workers made it impossible for anyone to fail." The person may simply be choosing to not draw attention to herself.

However, self-denigrating, self-defeating statements are telltale signs of a deeper insecurity. There is evidence that the seed of self-doubt was planted long ago, in one's childhood, and has reared its ugly head through conflict with a bully. All of us have doubts at one time or another, but most believe that we are inherently capable of overcoming obstacles. Those with historical doubts are always more susceptible to spiraling into despair whenever confronted by powerful people who only criticize and demean them.

It's one thing for the horrific bully to put down the Target, but when she does it to herself, it's painful to witness. For instance, it hurts to hear someone say:

"I only slow the others down."

"I never was good at this sort of thing, not good at anything really."

"You all should go on, I can't help. I'd only make it worse for you all."

"I never learned how to do computers. My kids are much smarter than me. I'm such a dolt."

"You may be right that I screw up a lot, but I'll try harder next time."

In addition, there are aspects of speech that provide nonverbal clues to a hovering predator. Relevant paralinguistic cues (all aspects of speech except the words themselves) include tone of voice ("mousy", timid), rate of speech (either slow enough to be interrupted or too fast and flurried to mask a fear of being detected as less than competent), and showing a tolerance for interruptions by the bully, all combine to convey a general lack of confidence.

Vulnerability Through Action

The way the Target walks, carries herself, sits, stands, uses hands, and uses interpersonal space is scrutinized by the bully, perhaps without the Target's awareness. Fear or intimidation can be signaled by a hesitant walking pace, short stride or actually walking backwards to attend to what the more powerful person is saying. Confident people typically gesture with their hands to punctuate speech. The absence of gestures does not necessarily indicate poor confidence. It does, however, convey a reticence either learned in a family that discouraged free expression or a deliberate delay in taking action. In either case, the bully pounces on the quiet, non-expressive person, assuming that she will not fight back when attacked.

Finally, bullies exploit personal space to their advantage. They stand too close, hover over your shoulder in your cubicle when your back is turned, and touch you to signify control rather than compassion. Whenever a Target fails to back the bully off, to re-establish a comfortable distance, she risks having the invasion of her personal space wreak havoc over her own sense of control. Cowering or tolerance of invasion often indicates submission to the bully.

The Campaign Survey Says . . .

1 Reason For Being Bullied

Target's refusal to be subservient,
to not go along with being controlled
(reported by 31% of respondents)

Bold, Best & Brightest

Paradoxically, bullies also target strong people for assault. Remember that bullies are, by nature, creatures haunted by their own inadequacy. On one level, they realize this, but the public persona they present is a mask of bravado and superiority. Rather than undertake an introspective analysis and personal re-socialization plan (as if one could redo childhood later in life to get it right), bullies prefer to lash out at others who threaten their presumption of superiority.

Into their work world come genuinely bright, creative, self-assured people. Since these people are a threat, bullies work hard to undermine them.

They sabotage them through a myriad of covert means. They spread rumors and misrepresent the accomplishments of this group of Targets. If the bully is a subordinate or co-worker, the rumor mill of disinformation is the only means by which the desperate bully can claw her way back into control.

If the bully is the boss of the Bold, Best or Brightest, all she has to do is constrain the Target's creativity, pile on impossible burdens, or steal credit for the Target's work. These Target types will leave the job or stay to outwit the bully because, thanks to their self-confidence, they have a low threshold for the lies bullies dish out.

If the bright Target chooses not to compete with the bully, she could be untracked and walk away from a job in disbelief about the banishment. All she wanted was "to be left alone to do the job I was hired to do, as best as I could do it." There is a naivete about these Targets. They are highly proficient in the work to be done, but oblivious to office politics (the sole reason to exist according to the bully's world view).

The Campaign Survey Says . . .

#2 Reason For Being Bullied

"Bully Envy" of the Target's skill, knowledge or
ability to work with people
(reported by 21% of respondents)

Workplaces That Mentor Bullies

Good Employers Purge Bullies
Bad Ones Promote 'Em

Much is made about the role of workplace culture in determining the level of satisfaction or dissatisfaction an employee experiences. Of course, the culture may be as sprawling as the company is large. Or culture can be contained within a single work group of employees under the control of one supervisor.

Companies and agencies whose main characteristic is denial about any problems, gives itself the chance to avoid ever addressing problems because they simply do not exist. People addicted to drugs think like this. In Anne Wilson Schaef and Diane Fassel's classic *The Addictive Organization*, the point is amply illustrated that firms can operate with a common mindset not unlike that of an addict.

Denial of problems: "we may have a minor problem, but not a major one"

Confusion: from trying to predict what will happen next and how to deal with it

Dishonesty: it is more about "packaging" and putting on a good front

Perfectionism: pretending to know all solutions

Illusion of Control: where feelings are seen as weaknesses

Scarcity principle: encourages hoarding, getting more for yourself, cutthroat behavior

Ethical Deterioration: a spiritual void from the habits of lying, cheating & stealing

Screwed-up Communication:

- ☐ Indirect—talking about a person through others rather to that person

- ☐ Abundant, but ineffective—lots of memos, but little is learned from them and the messages are not to be trusted

- ☐ Secretive—about salaries, promotions, hiring, etc. "for their own good"

- ☐ Skilled incompetence—being meeting'd to death, constant planning, no action

- ☐ Preference for Logical, Rational, Dualistic style supposedly the facts only, black or white only

Poor Thinking:

- ☐ Bad memory—lessons never learned, mistakes repeated

- ☐ Tolerance for Individuals Dumping on Others—instead of working out personal problems

- ☐ Norm of Dishonesty—based on the belief that in the organization, one can't succeed if honest

- ☐ Judgmental—people become bad, not their ideas or performance, a dread of evaluations

- ☐ Crisis Orientation—distracts from doing routine work, initially exhilarating, but eventually exhausting

❏ Forcing People to Take Sides on Issues—encourages co-dependent behavior

In workplaces characterized by the above list, an Opportunistic bully could practice her craft without calling attention to
herself. The company becomes the bully's accomplice. We know
from our survey results that employers were seen as playing a
vital role in sustaining, even if not directly contributing to, the
bullying.

This finding parallels the "hostile work environment" basis
for sexual harassment charges. Any workplace that fosters bullying is certainly hostile.

The Campaign Survey Says . . .

Targets Divide Responsibility for Bullying

Bullies: 59.5% responsible
Employer: 24%
Law/Society: 8.3%
Targets: 8.2%

Chapter 3
Targethood, An Undeserved Burden

*That's what it takes to be a hero, a little gem of
innocence inside you that makes you want to
believe that there still exists a right and wrong,
that decency will somehow triumph in the end.*
                                        - Lise Hand

Chapter preview:
Recognizing bullying
Crazymaking
How you could not notice
Healthy self-denial
Origins of self-denial
Denial cycles
Prolonged denial worsens situations
A word about control
The many faces of hurt
    Emotional-psychological effects
    Physical illness
    Stages of stress
    Stress is real
    Symptoms of stress
PTSD
What to do

Recognizing Bullying

Check all the following that apply.

__ 1. Your co-worker or supervisor seems irritated or
angry with you at least two times a week, although you always try your best to do your work
on time and well.

__ 2.   You often feel confused because she responds to your work efforts with criticism even when you have tried your hardest to do things "her" way.

__ 3.   You are upset with your working relationships. Your attempts at communication are constantly misunderstood and degraded.

__ 4.   You constantly wonder "What's wrong with me?" "No matter how hard I try to please her, I always feel that I have done something wrong."

__ 5.   She rarely includes you in her plans for work although she expects you to fully understand what she wants you to do.

__ 6.   She is either angry or "doesn't know what you are talking about" when you try to discuss work issues with her.

If you agree with 2 or more of these statements, you are probably bullied at work.

Just as the frog in a pot slowly brought to boil underestimates the danger he faces, bullies lull Targets into their traps with an initial approval that gives way to naked aggression over time.

As bad as being bullied feels, it is natural to downplay its impact on your life for many reasons.

Crazymaking

Bullying is crazymaking. If you feel this is happening to you, check the following list of situations that highlight crazymaking tactics. These come from the book *Stop! You're Driving me Crazy* by George Bach and Ronald M. Deutsch.

1. Feeling temporarily thrown off balance and momentarily unable to right oneself.
2. Feeling lost, not knowing where to turn, searching aimlessly.
3. Being caught off guard.
4. Feeling disconnected, confused, disoriented.
5. Feeling off balance, as if the rug had been pulled from under your feet.
6. Receiving double messages but somehow unable or fearful to ask for clarification.
7. Discovering that you were mistaken in your evaluation of where you stand or what is currently the status quo.
8. Feeling unprepared for a broken promise or unfilled expectation.
9. Experiencing the shattering of an important dream.
10. Where you assumed goodwill, ill will seems to prevail.
11. You feel pushed around, not in control of your own direction.
12. What seemed clear becomes muddled.
13. You have an uneasy, weird feeling of emptiness.
14. You have a strong wish to get away, yet you feel unable to move, as if you were frozen.
15. Feeling vaguely suspicious that something is wrong.

You may have felt some or all of the above feelings at one time or another. These examples of bullying are not to be taken lightly. Bullying is hostile aggression. It is emotional abuse. Bullying can kill you with stress.

How You Could Not Notice

Is it possible to not know that you are the target of a bully's assaults? As odd as it sounds, yes. Self-denial allows it to happen.

Denial is a process we use to protect ourselves from something (bullying) that we think is so personally threatening that we could be immobilized if we face it head-on. Denial blocks our awareness of a painful reality.

It is important to realize that denial in its various forms is not deliberately deceitful. It is automatic. It is a useful unconscious safety-valve operation that the mind invokes to keep from being overwhelmed by circumstances.

Denial is adopted by individuals, both Targets and bullies, groups, work units, entire organizations and even nations. For brevity here, let's talk only about the Target's denial, a self-denial of an unacceptable, painful reality. Co-workers and the organization itself use the same techniques.

The term "denial" encompasses many forms that serve to protect us. All involve self-talk, adopting a script that when repeated serves to convince our own minds that the denial is the right thing to do. Some common forms are:

Simple denial

Maintaining that bullying is not happening despite evidence that it is and that it is also perceived by others. This is the "see, hear and speak no evil" approach. When the group discusses what the bully does, you leave the room, believing that when it is out of sight, it will be out of your mind.

Minimizing

Admitting to bullying, but downplaying it in such a way that it appears to be much less serious than it is. The lines "tough times build character" and "I have to grow a thicker skin, that's all" run through your mind.

Rationalizing

Offering other reasons or justifications for the behavior of the bully. To make the insane appear normal, you convince yourself that the bully's tactics are somehow justified. This leaves the Target with no one to blame but herself. "I must have done *something* to cause her to launch on me."

Intellectualizing

Avoiding the hurtful effects of the bully by dealing with it on the basis of generalization, intellectual analysis, or theorizing. This is the "macro" approach. The justification sounds something like: "Worldwide competition has driven my company offshore," or, "I'm lucky to have a job at all." or, "The pressure the poor CEO feels is more than a person should bear." How about, "His anxiety trickles down to the bully who is only mimicking how he is treated." You think, "She has no choice, she's merely going with the flow." or finally, "I have to accept a lean and mean environment so the company can remain competitive, because this is an economic necessity."

Healthy Self-Denial

When we are hurting from the effects of bullying and we feel vulnerable, we want the pain to stop. When we feel threatened or vulnerable after yet another round of bullying, it is sometimes important to deny the situation. It is too much to comprehend all at once. It's as if we are wearing a blindfold. We refuse to take it off to see what has happened.

This often works in the short term so we can finish what we need to do. It helps you limp to the planned vacation, to time off. When you are ripped by the boss, you use denial to get through the afternoon until you can get home and verify her craziness with your family and friends.

Without denial, the trauma from bullying could overwhelm you and render you inactive and immobile. Losing a job or constant harassment from a boss or co-worker can lead to shock. Denial is the defense we use to avoid the flooding of emotions after the initial shock wears off.

Everyone uses some sort of denial when in pain. If you come from a background where there was a lot of pain, you may have learned to use denial often to escape that pain.

Origins of Self-Denial

In the Target's family-of-origin, no one calls bullying what it is. The bully herself encourages and sustains denial by everyone.

In childhood, you may have often heard the words "You have nothing to cry about." This teaches the Target to not trust her feelings. When someone denies your right to feel and express a genuine emotion that you feel, it is called discounting. Having one's personal perspective disregarded while growing up explains why Targets would accept similar verbal taunts from the bully. Adult Targets simply do not trust or value their own version of events. Bullies always try to invalidate what you know to be true.

When the bully is confronted about her unacceptable behavior, she may say it never happened or that the Target "provoked" it. The Target who thinks she has no right to dispute those lies may instinctively search for a rational explanation, believing the bully has a logical reason for acting as she did. She may think "There must be some reason she is mad at me." or "If she thinks my work isn't good, it probably isn't."

The Target spirals into a trap of self-defeat, acting on a script rehearsed since childhood. The bully's work is perpetuated by the Target herself.

The Target's belief that the bully is behaving logically is one of the main sources of confusion. The bully may bring her an important work project and calmly explain what is to be done, only to be screaming at her when it is not done in 10 minutes. This rapid change from rational to irrational behavior increases the Target's confusion, driving the logic-hungry Target to look for sanity in an insane world. Denial minimizes pain from the confusion.

The Target may never have asked the question, "Am I being bullied?"

Many people have never heard of bullying and they do not know what it is. In many cases, the concept is totally new to them. It is amazing how many people have said to us that just having a name, a label, for what they were going through helped them start to do something about it. It helps pierce the veil of secrecy and shame imposed by bullies.

Denial postpones putting a name to intolerable mistreatment, which delays counterattacking.

Bullying is wrong because of the unilateral decisions bullies make. Targets do not invite, provoke, desire, approve of, prosper as a result of, the bully's assaults.

Bullying Is NOT The Target's Fault!

Daily torment from a bully also encourages self-denial by Targets. She is told that she is too sensitive, too competitive, and trying constantly to have her own way. It is like brainwashing and can even extend beyond work to encompass her family and her life.

Denial Cycles

Denial can come and go after bullying as a way to avoid acknowledging pain. This is demonstrated by psychologist Lenore Walker who has researched domestic violence. Her model of the cycle of abuse from domestic violence fits well with the concept of bullying.

Applying Dr. Walker's model to the work world goes like this: first, everything seems to be going well at work. Then, tensions begin to rise as the Target experiences stress from the bully's undermining tactics. This is then followed by a verbal, destructive incident of bullying, causing Target confusion. She wonders how she can change herself to make her boss or co-worker happy. The Target's attempts to change (to meet the bully's standards) to appease the bully are at first met with approval. Things around the office are quiet for a while—until the bully feels out of control, and then the cycle begins again.

For the cycle of bullying to stop, denial must be broken. The Target must recognize the bullying, to begin to intervene on her own behalf. Taking control of your life and your destiny is the only way to stop Bullying.

Prolonged Denial Worsens Situations

Denial is acceptable as a short-term strategy only. While the Target is in denial, she remains stuck in circumstances of her mind's invention that prevent a realistic assessment of the situation. Without taking that first appraisal step, no action to restore dignity at work can or will be started. Prolonged denial is a dead-end.

Psychologist Jerry Harvey, author of *The Abilene Paradox and Other Meditations on Management* (see Chapter 5), blames the overreliance on denial on people's overblown *negative fantasies*. That is, they imagine the worst possible, albeit unlikely, outcome from confronting the bully—they would lose their jobs, the bully would turn on them, they would have a heart attack, the bully would kill their children, and so on. With a mind full of negative thoughts like these (mostly about events that would never occur) individuals act very conservatively. People want to take no risk.

Our aversion to risk coupled with an exaggerated imagination that limits thinking about possibilities allows the Target-bully relationship to grow even stronger with time.

Further, the longer a confrontation with the source of your pain at work is postponed, the less likely that action ever taken will stop the bully. Prolonged denial is a form of distraction which over time, actually loses its only usefulness—the power to mask depression and self-doubt.

> ## Ironic Reality: *Failing To Confront* Costs A Procrastinating Target and Family More Than The *Wprst imagined* Consequences Of Confronting

A Word About Control

Control is the central underlying theme, the ultimate basis of bullying. Dealing with the chaotic co-worker or boss, the out-of-control corporate environment, and the rigid rules of the business world are all closely linked to the theme of control.

The need for control is always there. Worries about losing control are the core issue for both Targets and bullies.

For the Target, the need for control is great. The fear of appearing too open, too needy, too aggressive, too angry is linked to every aspect of work. Seen from the other side, control means being dominant, demanding, aggressive and totalitarian. Targets believe that the only way to protect themselves is to maintain control. The issue becomes black-or-white. This emphasis on control leaves the Target vulnerable to bullies who start the entire bullying melodrama in order to appease their own need for control.

Stephanie Brown, in her book *Safe Passage: Recovery for Adult Children of Alcoholics*, draws a distinction between coping and being defensive. She states that coping creates problems in that situations (with bullies) are never resolved. Thus, using denial as a coping strategy only leads to bigger and bigger problems. It never solves the problem. Without resolution of some sort, Targets find their pain prolonged indefinitely.

The Many Faces of Hurt

Bullying Can Be Hazardous To Your Health
It Causes Psychological INJURY
Targets Are Not Mentally Ill!

Bullies affect Targets both psychologically and physically. Remember that psychological effects are to be taken seriously. They can kill as easily as heart attacks. Uncontrolled depression can trigger suicide faster than it takes to develop heart disease. So, know that the emotional-physiological effects listed below also threaten a person's health.

Psychological pain should not be minimized or denied by Targets or others. Stoic bravery or toughness are no match for suicidal thoughts or feelings of terror when you turn into the company parking lot in the morning. Seek help. You owe it to yourself and the people who love you. They recognize and want the very real pain you endure from bullying to stop.

The greater the severity of psychological pain, the more dangerous and the longer the effects seem to last.

Let's order the effects from mild to severe within each category.

Emotional-Psychological Effects

- Poor concentration, forgetfulness
- Stress, anxiety, irritability
- Mood swings, bursts of anger
- Spontaneous crying, lost sense of humor
- Indecisiveness
- Social withdrawal from co-workers, friends & family
- Panic attacks, depression
- Feelings of insecurity, being out of control
- Nightmares about the bully
- Obsessive thinking about the bully
- Always anticipating the next attack (on-alert status, vigilance)
- Loss of sleep, fatigue (number one factor in workplace accidents)
- Shattered faith in self-competence and feelings of worthlessness
- Shame, embarrassment, and guilt (which preserves the silence bullies require to thrive)
- PTSD (Post-Traumatic Stress Disorder, detailed below)

- Violence resulting in death. If PTSD or prolonged clinical depression goes untreated, the results are suicide, severe retaliation against the bully, or violent rage against anyone unfortunate enough to be nearby

Physical Illnesses: Mild to Fatal

- Reduced immunity to infection: more colds, flu
- Menstrual difficulties
- Itching, skin disorders
- Stress headaches
- Increased allergies, asthma
- Indigestion, colitis, irritable bowel syndrome
- Rheumatoid arthritis
- Hair loss
- Hyperthyroidism: overactive thyroid gland
- Migraine headaches
- Hypertension: high blood pressure.
- Diabetes mellitus
- Peptic ulcers
- Heart palpitations
- Coronary thrombosis: heart attack
- Micro-shredding: Heart attack from long-term stress

This last, and most threatening illness was defined by Robert S. Elliot MD, a cardiologist hired by NASA to find out why many of their young engineers were dying mysteriously. It was determined that they had experienced Micro Shredding (stewing) of the heart muscle caused by stress.

An old phrase in America is "Stewing in your own Juices" meaning that the person was under such duress, stress, and anger that he is stewing his body. The symptoms are a sudden burning sensation of "heartburn" that is not due to gases in the stomach.

What really happens is that the person is experiencing a special type of heart attack caused by excessive long term stress.

Dr. Elliot discovered that NASA had employed a Negative Incentives policy in the workplace. At the end of every successful rocket project, NASA terminated 15% of the engineers. This policy caused deep anxiety within an engineer's mind that he or she could contribute to project's success and yet be part of the group to be terminated.

As the study found, this type of anxiety caused many heart failures. Age, incidentally, was not a factor as many of these engineers were in the 30-40 year age group.

Stages of Stress

The bully is the source of the Target's stress, the Stressor. It is the responses of your body and mind to stressors that determines the extent of damage inflicted. The sequence of biological stress is well known. There are three stages, as described by Hans Selye:

1. *Alarm* — the turning on of the body's defense systems, (designed to be brief) that affects the entire body—it enables the "flight or fight" response in the face of danger—physical or psychological. Unfortunately, the body reacts to fright from the impending pounce of a tiger the same way it does to an insult from the bully. Alarm triggers the sympathetic nervous system that releases adrenaline to deal with the stressor.

2. *Resistance* — the maintenance of an alert stage that usually stops after the alarm. The body expects, and needs, this reaction to be turned off so that normal functions can resume. Resistance to the bully however is continuous, and that depletes the body's defenses. If you stay in resistance

too long, the body rebounds and the actual damage occurs even when the stressor is gone.

3. *Exhaustion* — a full system breakdown, mentally and physically. It demands that the stressor be removed or it will claim your life. To get to exhaustion, you have to ignore all the warning signs that your body gives you (see above psychological and physical effects). These can lead to death if the stressor never disappears and the body and mind continues to fight indefinitely.

Stress Is Real

(Source of stress facts-American Institute of Stress)

✓   Job Stress is far and away the leading source of stress for adult Americans. 78% of Americans describe their jobs as stressful.

✓   75-90% of visits to primary care physicians are for stress-related problems.

✓   The National Safety Council estimates that 1 million employees are absent on any average workday because of stress-related problems.

✓   Job stress is estimated to cost American industry $200-300 billion annually, as assessed by absenteeism, diminished productivity, employee turnover, accidents, direct medical, legal, and insurance fees, Workers' compensation awards, etc. Put into perspective, that's more than the price for all strikes combined, and the total net profits of the Fortune 500 companies.

✓   60 - 80% of accidents on the job are stress related. 40% of worker turnover is due to job stress.

✓   Workers' compensation claims for job stress have skyrocketed; California employers shelled out almost $1 billion for medical and legal fees alone.

> *One reporter asked us why we take Targets at their word. "Aren't you concerned that they are making it up?" was her concern. Why would they? People lie about beauty, wealth and health. There is no reason to fabricate a tale about strokes, heart attacks, immobilizing anxiety.*

Symptoms of Stress

Here are some very common signs of a stress reaction in a traumatized person.

Physical Indicators

- Nausea, tremors of the lips, hands
- Feeling uncoordinated
- Profuse sweating
- Chills
- Diarrhea
- Dizziness
- Rapid heart beat
- Chest pain (have an MD examine you)
- Rapid breathing
- Increased blood pressure

- Muscle aches
- Uncontrollable crying
- Headaches

Thinking-Cognitive Indicators

- Mental slowness or confusion
- Indecisiveness
- Trouble with problem solving
- Time/place disorientation
- Poor concentration
- Memory problems
- Difficulty naming objects
- Nightmares
- Little-to-no attention span
- Self-blame
- Minimizing the experience
- Sense of an unfair world

Emotions as Indicators

- Anxiety
- Fear
- Guilt
- Grief
- Depression
- Sadness
- Feeling lost, abandoned or isolated
- Wanting to hide
- Anger
- Feeling shocked
- Numbness
- Wild mood swings
- Shame

The Campaign Survey Says . . .

Top 8 Effects of Bullying on Targets
1. Stress, anxiety
2. Depression
3. Exhaustion
4. Insecurity, self-doubt
5. Shame, embarrassment, guilt
6. Obsessive thinking, nightmares
7. Poor concentration
8. Sleeplessness

Harvey Hornstein, author of *Brutal Bosses and Their Prey*, surveyed nearly a thousand people for his book. Especially interesting were the health consequences for people subjected to disrespect. There were meaningful (& statistically significant) correlations between disrespect and depression ($r = .64$), anxiety ($r = .58$), and the loss of self-esteem (self-respect) ($r = .45$). Even more shocking is the long term harm done, defined by the PTSD experience.

PTSD

The American Psychiatric Association recognizes a condition called acute stress disorder with symptoms that include disorientation, confusion, intense agitation, and dazed detachment, sometimes followed by amnesia. This reaction apparently makes the development of PTSD more likely. The risk is also high when the stress is sudden, unexpected, and severe, or prolonged and repetitive, humiliates the victim, or destroys the victim's community and social support system. This is what bullying does!

Post-traumatic stress disorder (PTSD) is the injury that results from an overwhelming assault on the mind and emotions. A trauma is an event beyond the range of ordinary human experience — something that would be overwhelmingly terrifying for almost anyone. Even hearing about the suffering of another person is sometimes enough. Bullying often qualifies as a trauma, repeated over time.

The immediate response to a trauma can be intense fear, helplessness, or horror. The reaction may be delayed by days, weeks, months, or even years and last for a long time. There are three classes of symptoms:

(1)   Hyper-alertness: people are often edgy, irritable, easily startled, and constantly on guard, sleep poorly, become easily agitated, have trouble concentrating, are aggressive and easily startled

(2)   Thought Obsessions: involuntary re-living of the traumatic event in the form of memories, nightmares, and flashbacks that may recreate the responses and feelings of the actual event, or even act as though the event were recurring (these episodes may or may not be recalled), anxiety symptoms when exposed to anything that resembles, recalls, or symbolizes some aspect of the trauma,

(3)   Emotional Flatness: a need to avoid feelings, thoughts, and situations reminiscent of the trauma, a loss of normal emotional responses, feelings that seem unreal.

Not caring about the ordinary business of life, feeling cut off from the concerns of others, an inability to trust others.

Sensing that there is no future, anger at those responsible for the traumatic experience while simultaneously ashamed of their own helplessness, or guilty about what they thought or did or failed to do. Demoralized and isolated.

Numbing serves to suppress anger that might lead to an explosion of violence. No longer able to use their feelings as cues to pay attention to their needs, trauma victims habitually respond either too intensely or not at all.

With understanding and the support of loved ones the stress reactions usually pass more quickly. Occasionally the traumatic event is so painful that professional help may be necessary. This does not mean the person is weak. It simply indicates that the particular traumatic event was just too powerful for that person or any reasonable person to manage alone. Isolation is the enemy. Asking for help is essential.

Treating PTSD

Borrowing from the suggestions of William Wilkie, M.D. in the Australian book *Bullying from Backyard to Boardroom,* we propose treating PTSD using the following method.

1. The foremost thing to do is to **reassure the Target that she did nothing to cause her own victimization.** She is not to blame. The most severe damage a bully can cause is to undermine the individual's confidence in her competence. Targets often blame themselves for the bullying, for lacking courage, for being weak or for feeling defective when hurt by criticisms (however unwanted, unprovoked and undeserved). Above all, the Target is to be held blameless.

2. Assure the person that she is an *injured* person, not a men-
    tally ill one. She should receive treatment for the injury
    just as certainly as if she had fallen and broken an arm at
    work. She's not crazy.

3. Targets do not have to find a rational meaning for the bully's
    inane actions. If no reason can be found, she might have to
    come to grips with the reality that the bully's behavior is
    unwarranted and irrational and *makes no sense* (see Chap-
    ter 4).

The Campaign Survey Says . . .

The Target's Emotional Instability Persists
Survey respondents were divided into
- Short-term (≤ 1 year since bullying stopped)
- Longer-term groups (18 mos. to 10 years)

81.25% of short-termers still had frequent or
constant intrusive thought about the bullying

23.5% of long-termers suffered similarly

58% of all those who completed the Aftermath survey
said they were still troubled by bullying.

All trauma should heal with time as long as the Target ac-
knowledges that she is not to blame and starts the road to recovery. Be aware that events and circumstances that prolong
trauma and a return to pre-injury functioning include battling

interfering physicians, stupid lawyers, disbelieving colleagues, doubting family members, and defamatory references that find their way to the next employer.

What to Do

To alleviate the emotional pain:

Contact friends, don't stay alone, don't fight recurring thoughts (they are normal), eat well-balanced and regular meals, stay physically active, talk and write about what happened (create a journal, don't keep it bottled up), avoid stimulants (caffeine, sugar, nicotine), hug loved ones, use prayer/meditation, practice your faith, take hot baths, eat foods with tryptophan (warm turkey, baked potatoes, cream soups), play music.

What Family & Friends can do:

Listen patiently and carefully, spend time with the person, offer unsolicited help with daily tasks, reassure the person about being safe, don't take expressed anger personally, don't tell her that she is "lucky" it wasn't worse (say that you are sorry that the bullying ever occurred and that you want to understand and help).

Be sure to read Chapter 6 to learn a great deal
more about what to do.

Chapter 4
Irreconcilable Differences

There is overwhelming evidence that the higher the level of self-esteem, the more likely one will be to treat others with respect, kindness and generosity.

- Nathaniel Branden

Chapter preview:
Control is the issue
The controller
The cooperator
The inevitable collision
What's yours is mine, too

Many people who find themselves the target of a bully wonder why? Why is this happening to me?

Control Is The Issue

The foundation for all bullying is the concept of control. Whether you are a Target or a bully, you have to deal with control. The problem lies with the definition of "control." Bullies and Targets see control in two different ways. It is this difference which creates bullies who mistreat Targets.

We all start out at the same point. As babies we exist in a world where we are under the complete control of our parents. We benefit from this control to learn how to talk, walk, and function in society. Our different experiences in life define whether or not we become Targets or bullies.

As briefly stated in Chapter 3, the need for control exists for many of us. For Targets and bullies, the issue of control is vastly different. The Target operates as if surrounded in a world full of examples of cooperation.

The bully is desperate to dominate. The bully feels powerless, she only values herself when she is in control. She works in a reality that says she is only in control when she controls others. She avoids feeling powerless by flexing her control muscles. The more "exercise" she gets for that muscle, the less secure she is feeling.

The Controller

The bully lives, eats, sleeps and lives for control. She never really experiences life any other way. Living and success for her, *is* to control others with power. The power she has is both in title and her ability to generate fear and chaos in a work group.

The Campaign Survey Says . . .

89% of Bullies are Bosses

The bully never experienced the security of self-acceptance and cooperation in childhood that allows for adult cooperation. Because this was lacking, the bully was left insecure. With little self-acceptance, she developed intense feelings of powerlessness and worthlessness.

There is an Oz-like quality to a bully. Because of her inherent insecurity, she requires the smoke and mirrors presentation that the Wizard used in the Emerald palace of Oz. Remember the wizard's debunking? Toto pulled back a curtain that revealed a little shriveled-up man working the levers of his great-man illusion machine. Bullies are illusion artists. It's all appearance, no genuine substance.

Bullies are ignorant of their deficiencies. This comes either from a lack of insight or a denial of the consequences of her behavior. She denies abusing or attempting to control others. Instead, she prefers to fabricate a hokey story that the Target "provoked and deserved" a verbal tirade.

Bullies are:
- ❑ unpredictable
- ❑ angry
- ❑ intense
- ❑ sullen
- ❑ critical
- ❑ jealous
- ❑ manipulative
- ❑ explosive

Bullies have no intention of being in a "relationship" with their Targets. Normal relationships at work require give and take by both parties. The bully never admits to such humble interdependency. She may tell her Target that they are equal, but does this only to lull her into sharing secrets, habits and other private information which can be turned against her during attacks.

To be equal suggests inferiority to a bully. Equals have the right to reject one another. The bully hides a vulnerability to rejection, something she fears very much. As we said in the Chapter 14, a bully's anger, her raging public face, covers up pent-up fears from earlier times in her life.

Also in a relationship of equals, the bully would have to show feelings and ask for what she wanted (Chapter 13). She would eventually ask of others a question that could be answered "no." She abhors being on a level playing field like that.

Finally, there is a rebound effect that fiercely independent Targets experience. When that type of Target pushes the bully, the bully escalates her cruelty because the challenge to her control is so threatening. Remember, resistance to the bully's control was the #1 reason Targets believed they were bullied.

The Cooperator

The Target unknowingly smacks right into the wall of power and control projected by the bully. The most important moment for the Target is when she begins to question the rightness of the bully's behavior towards her. Depending on the difference in styles, it may take the Target a long while to acknowledge to herself that "something just isn't right." By then, family and friends question her unwitting tolerance of the bully's disrespectful mistreatment.

The Target and bully have opposing perceptions about control. The difference can be traced to their respective Families-of-Origin.

The Family-of-Origin is the biological family you were born into. The combination of heredity and parenting style within the family determined to a great extent how we behave as adults. Parenting styles affect the child's disposition (whether we become passive, hostile, or assertive) and our ways of relating to the world.

There are three main parenting styles: passive, autocratic, and egalitarian. Passive parents make few rules and tent to overprotect their children. Autocratic parents have strict and fast rules and allow little, if any, input from their children. Egalitarian parents use a more democratic approach towards childrearing, combining rule-making with input from their children.

Children who grow up in passive, overprotective, and strict families exhibit the shyness, reticence, and quietness that makes for an anxious adult in social situations. These same qualities make the children from these families unsure of their abilities, and thus, easy targets for bullies.

Parents who are overprotective keep their children socially naive because their overindulgent loving never allows their children to develop a realistic view of the world.

Autocratic parents never allow their children to behave in a way that differs from the parents. These children have an unrealistic view of the world, too. Because children of authoritative parents are repeatedly told what to do and how to do it, they become shy and quiet and show signs of withdrawal. These children are also less spontaneous and lack confidence in social situations. This sets them farther apart from other children and makes them an easy target for bullies.

One's Family-of-Origin affects the adult ability to solve problems. Through the daily routine of family life and the celebration of family events such as birthdays and holidays, the family is the place where we first learn to be social, to get along with others. If you are raised in a family where there is constant upheaval and there are no predictable rituals [such as meals or large family gatherings], you never develop the ability to have a normal interaction with others. The disruption of daily rituals in a child's life has profound impact because without the daily exposure to normal conversation, the child has little chance to begin learning the first steps of problem solving. Without the ability to problem solve, the child is an easy target for a bully.

Research from the area of addictions, gives another possible answer. It is clear that there are differences in children from alcoholic homes that allow some to grow up with more resilience than others. It is possible that this resilience is also what allows Targets to be able to learn to cooperate.

Targets as children are those who learn through the first two years of life that they don't have to use control to get what they need. Like the resilient children they are given much attention, no prolonged separation from a parent or caregiver, and they experience no overt parental conflict. (They may have problems, but these problems do not overwhelm the rest of their lives.)

They learn to use cooperation in a way that doesn't require winners or losers. They don't need to control anyone. They live and functions by collaboration. At work as an adult, they prefer an atmosphere that will foster cooperation and creativity.

Bullying is made possible by the failure of the Cooperator to realize the world is peopled by Controllers who do not have the Cooperator's best interest in mind.

The Cooperator-Target's naivete determines the size of the surprise when she finally realizes the Controller-bully's cutthroat nature.

Into the snakepit steps a Target who believes that colleagues at work will freely express their feelings, ideas and actively seek collaborative relationships. Because the job and good relationships define her work world, she assumes that that is true for everyone else including bullies. She loves her job, meaning the tasks that push her to employ her skills. Office politics are either ignored or considered of minimal importance.

Unfortunately, bullies see the workplace as a battlefield, a site to plunder others, home to the carnage that they consider unworthy adversaries who populate their work day and interfere with their divine right to unchallenged control over minions. Getting along is the farthest thing from a bully's mind. Politics is the sport of competitors. The spoils, literally the body count of those successfully dominated and devastated over the years, go to the bully.

The Inevitable Collision

It is disingenuous to characterize the clash between two such fundamentally different people a mere "personality conflict" or "miscommunication" or "misunderstanding." All those labels suggest that the Controller is willing to meet the Cooperator at least half way. This is not true.

As long as the Cooperator-Target keeps functioning under the rules of cooperation, she may believe that she is doing something "wrong." She will continue to turn herself inside out to please the bully who will never be appeased. The Target's healing cannot begin until she realizes the relationship with her bully is not normal. Once she starts doubting the bully instead of herself, she takes a step toward health.

Our portrait of a bully is sad. It turns horrific when we look at the pathological dance with an unsuspecting Target which is described in Chapters 1, 2 and 3. How could a Target fall into such a trap?

The answer is that Targets rarely see bullies coming. They simply see the world through a completely different lens.

Jill is a supervisor at a glass factory. She came to work at the factory after serving 10 years in the Navy. She prides herself on running a "tight ship" and has received commendations for her work as a supervisor. Sandy decided in high school that she wanted to work as an artist. She started her job in the glass factory immediately after graduation. After three months working under Jill, Sandy is ready to quit and give up her dreams.

What happened? Sandy walked right into a relationship with a controller. The following is an example of the relationship between the two women.

Jill comes into the break room and flops down in the chair at a table with Sandy and casually says to her. "Boy, are you a troublemaker."

Sandy, looking up, replies, "Why do you say that?" (Although she is surprised, she responds as though they are both operating under the same rules, a shared reality.)

Jill is now ready to begin the battle for control. To her, Sandy needs to understand that Jill is the SUPERVISOR. "The boss just vetoed your crazy idea to simplify the paint line." Jill says this with a touch of anger and a discernible note of triumph.

Sandy then feels she must defend herself. She says, "when I talked to you yesterday I was just discussing some ideas that I thought might help us work faster."

"Well I thought you wanted the boss to hear your idea. He did and he feels my way is better." In her mind Jill has won. She has used her control over Sandy to attack Sandy's basic perception of her abilities and herself.

Sandy is hurt and confused. She cannot seem to get Jill to understand that she only wants to help in their department. She is frustrated and doesn't seem to understand what Jill expected of her. She doesn't perceive Jill's need for control at all — because Jill often tells her that new ideas are important, this to Sandy, means mutual empowerment, not the control over others.

If Sandy had said "I feel hurt when you said I was a trouble maker," Jill, as a confirmed bully would have discounted her feeling by saying, "You're really blowing this out of proportion!" or (sarcastically) "Well, aren't you the poor thing."

Sandy would still be left feeling hurt and confused.

If Jill were in the reality of cooperation (Sandy's reality), she would have said, "Oh, I'm so sorry, I guess I should have talked more to you before I talked to the boss." In this case Jill could be accused of being crabby but she would then acknowledge her irritability.

Although Sandy operates under the reality of cooperation, she has no idea that Jill will *never* consult her about anything. Sandy has no idea that Jill functions with an entirely different mind set. Unfortunately, Sandy might never realize that Jill is not a cooperator, but functions in a hostile world of control.

What's Yours Is Mine, Too

There is another way to represent the contrast between Controller-bullies and Cooperator-Targets. It is a way of describing relationships that involves keeping score for the things that matter most to people. It's a model of social exchange that turns into exploitation.

Consider the Cooperator's world view with respect to keeping score in a game. Do you remember Mark McGwire's stated wish during the 1998 baseball season as he and Sammy Sosa eclipsed the all-time home run record? McGwire said he wished they could end the season in a tie. That statement was rare coming from a professional athlete whose world is dominated by competitors. For a brief moment, the world watched as competitors at the highest level of sports chased the record as friends, in public anyway, each wishing the other the best.

The ideal outcome for a Cooperator is to achieve a 50/50 split of the "goodies" (resources") that employees play for at work. Some cooperators have angelic souls and act the altruist. Altruists prefer to give to others. They would settle for giving the other person 100% of the resources, taking 0 for themselves. No one has spotted an altruist in the workplace in years. Call if you spot one. They are an endangered species in the competitive arena of business.

In the diagram on the facing page, the two end points on the horizontal line depict the altruist on the left (0/100 payoff), the Cooperator in the middle seeking common ground represented by the vertical line and the Controller at the right end of the line seeking a 100/0 payoff.

A Cooperator's optimistic world of equality
50/50 split

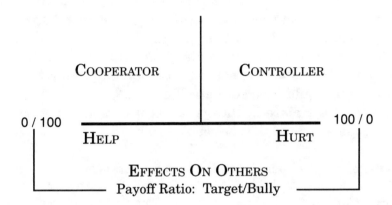

Controllers are strict competitors, zero-sum game players. Their winnings come at the expense of the other person's losses. The ideal outcome for a Controller is 100% for herself and 0 for the Target. Their logic: what's mine is mine and what's yours is mine, too. Note how in the second diagram the Controller (bully) cuts into the Cooperator's (Target's) half of the "goodies."

Bully exploitation of the Target's 25/75
split, on the way to 0/100 domination

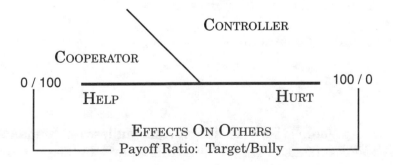

The Target-bully Tango in this exchange-exploitation model is a struggle between the two over the angle of the vertical line. The bully pushes from her side, trying to flatten the line, to achieve a 100/0 score. The Target is pushing back (once she realizes the exploitation she is suffering) just to get the line upright again. The Target does not think about pushing past the 50/50 mark into the Controller's turf. If and when she did go beyond the restoral of self-respect, beyond getting back to neutral, she would then see herself as a bully.

Instead of a place in the sports record books, we working stiffs trade "goodies" that become our payoffs.

Resources over which Controllers seek domination:

❑ Approval

❑ Credit for accomplishment

❑ Time (hours worked, free time)

❑ Supplies to do the job

❑ Authority on the job

❑ Respect

❑ Reputation with co-workers

Can you think of others?

The difference between Targets and bullies is as fundamental and cosmic as if Targets are from Venus, bullies are from Mars. Nah, it would never sell!

Chapter 5
Frozen Action

You gain strength, courage and confidence by every experience in which you really stop to look fear in the face ... You must do the thing you think you cannot do.

- Eleanor Roosevelt

Chapter preview:
Procrastinating
Catastrophizing
Action is the antidote
Why witnesses do not help
*   Abilene paradox*
*   Groupthink*
*   Dissonance*
*   Co-workers side with the bully*
*   Winners take all, Targets are losers*

A simple truth: to stop a bully from turning you into a Target, **just** firmly announce that her behavior (when she decides to test your resistance) will not be accepted without her running the risk that it will be reported immediately to both a private lawyer and company legal team. Gesture that she has one chance to stop now (palm of your raised hand facing her) and that she consider the consequences of continuing her childish, embarrassing behavior.

Easy to say, right? Easy to understand and dream about, too. But nearly impossible to do. If it were *just that simple,* you would have done it in the first place and skipped all the misery from being the bully's Target.

All the pain now felt as a Target comes not from that single missed opportunity alone, but from the postponement of taking action to right the wrong. Nipping it in the bud, people would call it. But using another old saying, it's all water under the bridge, the current situation requires you to stop the hurt however you can.

Procrastinating

Targets are trapped by bullies in a deliberate web of lies. The gravest danger comes when self-doubt begins to overwhelm the good employee. Over time, even the strongest person is worn down by constant verbal assaults.

Some Targets are surprised that another person, supposedly a fellow human being, could treat them so cruelly. These are people just wanting to do their jobs. The shock of having to react constantly to the uncompromising bully drains a great deal of their energy. Exhausted and disbelieving, they are unlikely to assert their rights effectively and renounce the bully.

In a way, bullies have much of the work done for them by veteran Targets. After the initial bully assaults planted the seeds of doubt, many Targets become their own worst enemies by staying wounded. The failure to mount a counteroffensive to put the bully back in her place sustains the suffering.

Targets may be too shocked or surprised to respond at first, but eventually fear freezes them. The don't seem to be able to take action to protect themselves. When friends and family ask why they are immobilized, several different-sounding reasons are offered, but fear explains them all.

"I love my job. It's the manager I can't stand. I will just stay away from her."

"I need major surgery in 6 months and have to have insurance benefits to pay for it."

"Some days are better than others. I can make myself invisible for a couple of weeks at a time."

"We are putting two kids through college and my wife doesn't work. I have to bring home a paycheck."

"I can tough it out. At least he's not as bad as the supervisor who left"

"No one in my family would understand my quitting. We've had only winners for generations. I can't quit."

Each of these people is more afraid of an unknown future in a different place, of doing different work than they are of the certain misery faced daily at the hands of their tormentor.

If these people would draw two columns, labeled Personal Costs of Doing Nothing and Benefits of Doing Nothing, they would see that costs far outweigh the benefits. (Review Chapter 3, the many faces of hurt).

Unfortunately, like an alcoholic who has to hit bottom before finding the motivation to change, Targets wait an incredibly long time before taking steps to purge bullies from their lives.

Catastrophizing

Worst-case thinking is to blame. Targets play disaster movies in their heads. The script for this melancholy movie features:

- Target complaints are met with indifference or rejection
- she feels no one listens to her or takes her seriously anymore
- the bully is made a hero by the company for her toughness and squeezing every ounce of productivity out of her staff
- family and friends threaten to abandon her
- the dog and cat sniff her and run, sensing a foul odor oozing from a day of clawing and fighting with the bully
- the bully steals her husband in the ending scene, leaving her homeless, unemployed and disabled with an appeal of a denied Workers' comp stress claim pending as the sun sets .... The End

This type of thinking is an illustration of how deep inside a Target's life a bully can get. The Target is the star, but the bully is the film's director.

Action Is The Antidote

Whatever you do, you need courage. Whatever course you decide upon, there is always someone to tell you you are wrong. There are always difficulties arising which tempt you to believe that your critics are right. To map out a course of action and follow it to the end, requires some of the same courage which a soldier needs.

- Ralph Waldo Emerson

Ask yourself: How can it be any worse than it already is? You answer "by being retaliated against." This is harassment heaped on top of harassment.

The point is that continued crap is guaranteed if nothing is done to stop the bully. Even if stopping the bully by complaining is unlikely, you cannot be certain until you try.

How Real Is Risk? Guaranteed Misery vs. A Chance For Peace Of Mind

The point is to ask yourself "what have I got to lose?"

The Campaign Survey Says . . .

When asked what they would have done differently, veterans of bullying wars said, in their own words:

I would have challenged the bully more and stood up for my own beliefs instead of backing down.

Take a stand and get the help you need to confront the bully because you wouldn't have a bully on your back if there were more people on your side.

Fight back from the beginning.

Realize that the bully is really a coward.

Why Team Members Do Not Help

The bully typically singles out one Target at a time. However, there are witnesses. Why do they watch and do nothing?

> ## TO THRIVE, BULLIES REQUIRE
> ## • Secrecy • Shame • Silent Witnesses
> ## You Can Stop Them
> ## Cut Off Their Life Support!

If groups (call them work teams) are powerful enough to bend individuals to their will, to get inside individuals' heads and make them doubt their own competence, to make them do things that hurt themselves, then logic would dictate that fellow workers who see a bully hurting someone would run to the rescue. Right? Wrong!

The strange tale of people acting in groups and influencing individuals now gets stranger. For many reasons, people witnessing the injustice of workplace bullying rarely act. They either will not act, by choice, or cannot act, for reasons often unknown to them and to the target who could certainly use their help.

Let's take a look at five common things that affect co-workers and witnesses of bullying which discourage them to intervene or help.

Abilene Paradox

Jerry Harvey honored his Texas roots when he named this phenomenon. The group dynamic is perhaps the most relevant to understanding why bullies can be witnessed by so many people and still get away with it.

The Texas city is the namesake for the paradox. It refers to the retelling by Harvey of a lousy decision by his family. On a hot summer day, the family piled into a car without air conditioning and drove too many miles to Abilene to try a new diner. The heat was oppressive; the food was lousy. But no one dared to speak in those terms until later that night back home.

Finally, the matriarch of the family broke the silence by complaining about the food. Then everyone chimed in with their complaint—the car was hot, it was stupid to try an unknown restaurant. It turns out that no one wanted to go in the first place, but no one said so when it mattered. Eventually, they all blamed the father for suggesting the drive.

To Harvey, whenever a group is about to do the wrong thing, despite knowing it's the wrong thing, it is a group "on the road to Abilene."

Imagine a committee of bright people making a stupid decision. We know from talking with each person alone that each and every one of them thinks it's a stupid thing they are about to do. When the committee votes, however, they choose to do the stupid thing anyway! Later, usually much later, when the decision backfires, the committee tears itself apart in its search for a culprit. The group desperately needs someone or something to blame, long after the very preventable decision was made.

This describes a group in agreement, not in conflict. They all agree privately, and individually, about the true state of affairs. They do not communicate their feelings to one another, however. Then publicly, in the presence of each other, they all deny the agreement that they don't know exists among them.

The paradox is that both the private and public versions of reality coexist. In fact, this is the mismanagement of agreement, not disagreement. It is all made possible by a public silence regarding what each individual knows to be true. Sound like where you work?

Take a bullying example. All the Target's co-workers know what is happening. If interviewed alone and free from retaliation, each would deplore the obvious pain the target is experiencing. However, in group settings, even without the bully present, they don't do the right thing.

When together, they don't plan how to use their group power to overcome a lone bully. Instead, they ignore the rampant mistreatment by not communicating their positions or feelings publicly. If the Target later pursues legal action and investigators on her behalf interview the team that made up the hostile environment, the finger pointing begins.

Why does this happen? Jerry Harvey traces it to people's overblown negative fantasies. That is, they imagine the worst possible, riskiest outcome from confronting the bully—they would lose their jobs, the bully would turn on them, they would have a heart attack, the bully would kill their children, and so on. We called this catastrophizing above. With a mind full of negative thoughts like these, mostly about events that will never occur, individuals act very conservatively as a group. As a group, they want to take no risk. So, they do the wrong thing, all for lack of talking about it openly. They let bad things happen to the Target that they believe, as individuals, should not happen.

Sick? No, simply human nature's aversion to risk, thanks to an exaggerated imagination that limits thinking about possibilities.

Silent, inactive witnesses to the bullying of others is a group "on the road to Abilene."

Groupthink

Groupthink is the second of five common workplace group dynamics that inhibit witnesses of bullying to intervene or help Targets.

This also involves groups making poor decisions such as allowing the bully to hurt people in the work team. In Groupthink, the wrong thing is done by the group, but they are not aware that it is wrong, as they were in the Abilene paradox.

Groupthink is George Orwell's term from *1984*, the dark futuristic (at the time) novel. Psychologists borrowed the term to describe a group incapable of critically assessing the pros and cons of decisions. Because the group members feel so tightly connected, so cohesive, they prefer to see only one side of an issue. They are easily led by a forceful leader and busy themselves falling in line behind the boss, kissing up to stay in good favor. They become a mindless, overprotective clique when assembled as a group, putting the political goal of squashing dissent above all other matters.

Groupthink is relevant to bullying if we imagine a management committee on which the bully sits. The Target tries to find an ally among the bully's peers. If and when she approaches group members, she will be given the cold shoulder. The management group will not be open to hearing complaints about one of their own. The bully is safe in her cocoon; the wagons are circled to protect a club member.

Little wonder that appeals for help to the bully's peers so frequently fail, from executive suite clubbies to shop floor buddies. Groupthink is designed to protect club members from hearing anything that contradicts their comfortable view of the world. It's the wall that separates the ingroup from all others. It carries with it a code of silence that plays into the bully's strategy.

Dissonance

Cognitive dissonance is the third of five common workplace group dynamics that inhibit witnesses of bullying to intervene or help.

Dissonance describes the emotionally-charged conflict that results from having two competing cognitions (beliefs) held by the potential helper. Let's get inside Sally's head in the story below. Leon Festinger is the psychologist most closely associated with this phenomenon called cognitive dissonance.

Chris and Sally were Helen's best friends during her short stay in the department. All were psychotherapists. Sally was the first to offer her friendship. Sally spent many lunch hours telling Helen horror stories about Zoe, Helen's terrifying boss. Zoe had chased out a man from Helen's position a year before and he was rumored to not have recovered from the stress Zoe caused.

Sally herself had transferred to another supervisor to escape Zoe's unpredictable rages and admired Helen's ability to get along with her. Chris had once held Zoe's position as boss, but gave it up after Zoe was hired as a staff therapist. Chris' life was made completely miserable trying to counter Zoe's political tricks and sabotage. So she abdicated and Zoe got her job, the one she wanted.

Chris confided in Helen that she was terrified of Zoe and managed to avoid contact with her as much as possible. She even took to hiding in her office until Zoe passed so she wouldn't have to face her in the hall.

Helen was later driven from the department by Zoe. Despite the similar experiences with Zoe by Chris and Sally, both refused to meet to comfort Helen after she left. Both left unanswered telephone messages left by Helen. Later, when Helen sued the corporation, Helen's attorneys interviewed Chris and Sally and concluded that their testimony would damage Helen's case as they both chose to support Zoe's position.

The most common way to reduce dissonance is to exaggerate the positives of one belief and the negatives associated with the alternative, so you can create a clearer choice of one over the other. For example, Sally could focus on the belief about the Helen's unfair banishment, but that could lead her to support Helen in court, risking good relations with Zoe, the tyrant.

Sally, like most people, chooses the path of least resistance. She decides to downplay the second belief and conclude that where she works isn't so miserable after all. She rationalizes to herself that she would have to be stupid to stay in such a place and she is not stupid. Therefore, Zoe's world with Zoe in it must not be so bad; Helen was wrong.

As with all these phenomena, we're simply trying to explain why people do not help more. Dissonance is not about morality. Once people rationalize away internal conflicts to make themselves feel good, the likelihood of them taking the humane, but more difficult, action decreases.

You can probably see how dissonance is related to siding with the bully. Since the survivor and bully are both still there, the survivor engages in a mental calculus of sorts to justify staying. She concludes, like Sally, that Zoe is more important than Helen who is gone anyway.

Co-Workers Side with the Bully

A fourth reason the team fails to use their group power to stop a bully is that team members side with the bully against the Target. The origin of the principle of identification with the aggressor is in psychoanalysis, but let's not get Freudian here.

What's important is that this explains how the Target's best friend or to the person who once stood as the Target's strongest ally can turn against her.

Most bullies want to torment the Target out of her job. The loyalty switching typically happens after the Target leaves. Without the painful daily reminders of the bully's devastating effect on the Target, their friend, co-workers are free in the aftermath to act as if the person were never there. They may buddy up to the bully more obviously to the observer, but without a personal awareness of what they are doing. The new-found loyalty to the bully may be borne out of fear to protect themselves, but to all observers, it looks like a choice made freely.

Sadly, after the Target is gone, former co-workers will dump on the Target, blaming her for her fate, for simply not understanding office politics or for having a "personality clash" with the bully. This rationalization protects the co-workers left behind at the expense of the departed Target.

Winners Take All; Targets Are Losers

Without the marvelous book *Winner Take-All Society* by Robert Frank and Philip Cook, we would have called this explanation Americans' love of competition. We revere winners and have no "mental shelf space" left for also-rans, the losers.

It is a pervasive marketplace mindset that has invaded our social relationships. The vast majority of riches go to the privileged few at the top of any profession, sport or hierarchy. In a way, the classic American competitive zeal encourages us to denigrate luckless Targets and elevate the bully. After all, if the workplace is war, the conqueror (even if she's a bully) gets the post-game interview while the vanquished retreats unnoticed and unloved.

Competition requires scarcity. There has to be a limited pool of possible rewards—monetary and social—over which workers have to fight. At work, social goodies can be as simple as civilized conversation, decent humane treatment, empathy for another's pain, and personal time given to someone who needs nothing more than the validation that companionship or an open mind can provide. These "resources" are not scarce. They are limitless.

Yet, the bully and her accomplices, by virtue of witnessing but taking no action, hoard them. By doling out praise and kindness in a miserly way, the bully controls the competition.

We naively refer to "free market" competition as if the game is fair. In fact the distribution of opportunities always tilts toward the powerful. In organizations, bullies control opportunists, those whom they designate as Targets don't have a chance.

It is unthinkable that we treat bullies decently at work, while ignoring the deliberate harm they cause to others. What we score as success is screwed up, too. We place a high value on the size of a person's workstation, type of chair, type of benefits for which she's eligible, window or interior cubicle, basement or penthouse office, day or graveyard shift, expense account or out of pocket, and so on.

Success is defined by relative standing rather than absolute performance. Companies blithely credit bullies with winning and treat Targets like losers. Hey, the game is rigged!

Chapter 6
Your Best Advocate

Freedom is the will to be responsible to ourselves.
- Nietzsche

Chapter preview:
What friends should tell Targets
Positive actions that help
Consumer's guide to "helpers"
 Employee assistance programs
 Union representatives
 Chambers of commerce: employee hazards
 Lawyers for employees only
 Work Doctor's lawyer interview
 The courts
 Dilbert® as proxy
Your best advocate is you

As mentioned earlier, before Targets typically call for help, a great deal of time has passed. Targets wait too long, erroneously thinking the problem is their fault. It is extremely important that Targets not be isolated. They should rely on, not distance themselves, from friends and family during these stressful times. Caring friends can help. Here's how.

What Friends Should Tell Targets

- they did not cause the bully to assault them. (If you think Targets invited harm from the bully, stop now. You will do more harm than good. Do NOT volunteer. Get a job in HR or EAP! You can't help!)

- bullying is the name for what they experienced.

- they are not likely the only Target of that bully's unreasonable behavior (they are probably not alone in the company).

- there are witnesses, perhaps silent at first, who may be enslisted to help combat the bully.

- shame and guilt are what the bully wants the Target to feel. Both are natural, but are useless. They delay recovery and healing.

- the Target's perceptions are real & acceptable. Being kind, bright or cooperative still matters most.

- she is not imposing on you by seeking help. People do want to right wrongs and help others.

- bullying is common at work (20-85% according to surveys, thus affecting millions of people).

- the bully's way of viewing the work world is perverted. The Target's perspective is not twisted.

Positive Actions That Help

> LISTEN without judging or evaluating
  - Avoid criticism.
  - Affirm, be positive.
  - Avoid asking "why?" the Target did what she reported. This puts the Target on the defensive and makes you seem an investigator, virtually an accomplice of the bully.
  - Be patient. Let the Target talk at her own pace. Do not interrupt or fill silent time with your talk. Do not finish sentences for the Target. Take a breath before you speak so you can be calm and deliberate. Put care into your voice. The floor belongs to the Target-you are to follow the lead.

> CONFIRM/VALIDATE the Target's reality
  - Assume the Target's perspective completely. Do not try to be "balanced" by stating both sides of the conflict between the Target and bully.
  - Use only as much information as necessary, based on a strict "need to know" basis. Sometimes simply putting a name to the experience is enough to start the healing process.

> SHOW EMPATHY
  Empathy is the ability to walk in someone's shoes and to feel what they feel.See the situation from her perspective. If you have had similar feelings, say so. If you have not, don't lie. Simply try to understand what it must feel like and convey that understanding.

➢ SHARE PERSONAL EXPERIENCES
> You would not have volunteered if you did not have a brush with bullying, either directly or vicariously through a family member. When appropriate, without imposing, try to tell your story, especially the part about moving on with one's life. You have the chance to be a source of hope. Seize it.

➢ EDUCATE
- Be current on the topic. Turn to the Campaign and other sources for information.
- Suggest actions to take—call the labor commissioner, ask co-workers about their experiences, call the Campaign for an attorney referral, plan an internal tribunal to bust the bully, visit a physician to document impact on health. Be an idea generator for the Target.

Consumer Guide to 'Helpers'

Employee Assistance Programs

EAP is a counseling program often provided by employers in addition to health insurance coverage that may or may not include counseling by a mental health professional.

EAPs were originally developed to treat employee alcoholism. In many medical plans, the broader scope of services now includes help for "job stress." Ideally, independent professional counselors are available off-site to visit on company time with no need for the employee to divulge to management the reason for the limited number of visits.

However, like every employer-provided benefit, EAPs come with strings attached. Here are some of the disturbing trends we have learned through direct experience and from visitors to our web site who report the following EAP traps for the unsuspecting employee.

- *Counselors are employees.* When counselors are no longer independent contractors, they become accountable to management and fall under company control. They lose their neutrality and ability to see oppression in the workplace. With employee counselors, employees with troubles will be seen as causing problems and loss of money for the company. Loyalty is given to the company that issues the paycheck. Ask who your counselor works for.

- *The company's preference for on-site locations.* This means that someone seeking relief from a bully boss has to seek help in an office visible to co-workers and the raging boss on the premises. Confidentiality is already compromised. Furthermore, on-site counselors' time is subject to exploitation by managers seeking "tips" for dealing with troublesome employees. So, instead of helping employees full-time, they spend teaching supervisors how to manage who nag them for help with "problem" employees.

- *Supervisor referrals are given priority.* Employees with problems should be able to refer themselves (self-referral) to counselors, when needed. However, supervisor referral, the most frequently used EAP service, demonstrates that management views counseling as punishment to "straighten out" the employee who doesn't agree to be subservient to a bad manager. Your job security may hinge on participating in mandatory counseling. This is an abuse of mental health services, undermines program effectiveness, and prostitutes counselors who cooperate.

- *Privacy invasions are on the rise*. Supervisor-referred clients, just like those mandated to do EAP following a dirty drug test, have few protections of their counseling record. Notes taken during an ostensibly confidential session should be off limits the management but observations are exchanged during informal conversations. Check to see exactly what information the company is entitled to require from your counselor. Ask your counselor. In legal cases, counselor notes can be dragged into public court for the employer to see. Even voluntary EAP clients risk invasions of privacy by granting complete access to medical records. Never sign a general release to the employer unless advised by your lawyer. The most horrific trend is that some radical insurance company representatives attend counseling sessions and direct the therapist about techniques used to reduce the number of sessions.

- *Peer counselors with dubious qualifications*. EAP began as alcoholism counseling done by recovering alcoholics who worked for the company. Some programs still favor peer counselors with less training and experience than outside, independent professionals. Of course, if your EAP counselor is an addictions specialist, he or she won't understand the impact sick workplaces will have nor will they necessarily be sympathetic to the complex effects of bullying, such as PTSD and other effects of stress, separate from chemical dependency. Ask your EAP counselor about credentials and experience with situations like yours.

Please take precautions when using an EAP.

Union Representatives

Unions, like employers, are organizations. They have agendas and goals that may or may not meet your needs. As incredible as this sounds, unions are not automatically good at giving unconditional employee support. Unions have appropriated the name "labor," but their influence extends to less than 15% of the American workforce today.

Exerpted cases from the The Work Doctor ® files:

Clara was a Teamsters union member schoolbus driver. Her boss was an old fashioned sexual harasser who monkeyed with her bus so that she lost her brakes with a load of children on board. When she called the union for help [the national union publishes the Teamsters guidelines clearly defining how the local union is supposed to defend harassed employee members], the rep called her a "fat, ugly broad not worth fighting for" and refused to see her.

Susan is the only female meat packer at a grocery store. She belongs to a union. Troubles with her immediate boss and the store manager led her to the union. In preparation, she wrote 18 questions she wanted answered about the reprehensible behavior of both bosses. The union rep scheduled only 30 minutes to hear her complaint. Halfway through the meeting after rolling his eyes in disbelief, he terminated the session. Susan protested so much that he scheduled a follow-up session the next day. Her husband accompanied her to that meeting. The rep was formally cordial and did start the formal grievance paperwork. When asked when they would get answers to Susan's 18 questions, the rep yawned and said "maybe never, there isn't time." Could they fax the list for him so he could find answers at his own pace, they queried. He refused. Only after Susan called the local union president, whose election she helped win, did the rep consent to read her questions.

I work for a steel mill. We have a local union. Recently our company has decided do away with all of our breaks. We work 8 hrs. a day and 40 hrs. a week. The company is saying that they are making us a continuous operation. They have not done this to the other departments. I have heard that there are laws that say that an employer has to give you a break after you work so many hours. We work 8 hours straight. They also moved one member of our group to another section and now we work with two people instead of three. And they are expecting the same amount of work. They are pushing us so hard. It is exhausting. Our union won't back us. They are letting the company do what they want to do.

Tara was bullied by a sexual harasser. She ran to the union and simultaneously to an independent employment lawyer. Her legal claim was postponed until the union grievance procedure was completed. She expected it to be weeks. Her case was a clearcut example of illegal sexual harassment. Once a month for a year, she called the union checking on the status of her grievance. They always put her off. Her lawyer could do nothing. TWO years later, a union rep called Tara to announce her hearing had been scheduled the next week. But she had returned to college and could not attend at the scheduled time. The rep said this jeopardized her claim. She called the local union president at home explaining her dilemma. He assured her that a new time could be set taking into account her class times. He told her to fax him her schedule. She did so. Weeks passed with no word of a new time for the hearing. Then, nearly two months after she first contacted the president, he called her to formally announce that her grievance had been dropped because she failed to appear at the hearing two months ago! He denied receiving

her faxed schedule and the conversation they had about reschedu-
uling.

It is a shame that young employees are ignorant of the positive role unions once played in improving working conditions. However, to reverse the rapid decline of union popularity, they will have to improve service to existing members. There is no excuse for the only official employee advocates to be too busy to help employees who seek relief from horrendous workplaces.

Beware of faux advocates! Several corporate-sponsored foundations and groups have large fund reserves and pose as friends of employees. Most are imposters. One such group is the National Right To Work Legal Aid Foundation. In 1997, they had 400 cases active in the courts to fight "union abuses" on behalf of employees. In reality, the only "abuses" they challenge are compulsory union dues of which a portion is earmarked for political action committees. The NRTW, a union-busting organization, is hardly the type of helper you need to get better service from your union.

If you feel that your union fails to protect your union rights for arbitrary, malicious, bad faith or discriminatory reasons, you can sue under the National Labor Relations Act. Consult a lawyer.

Chambers of Commerce: Employee Hazards

This national organization lobbies to forbid "frivolous" court action by mistreated and terminated employees while using the courts to stop OSHA from making America's most dangerous worksites safer for employees. Any contradiction here with "community service"?

As beltway insiders spun the Starr-Clinton-Jones-Lewinsky impeachment fiasco into an indecipherable mess, a stealth campaign of destruction likely to affect every hometown and every worker was underway. A wrecking crew had been silently amassing a fortune for a lobbying campaign to destroy the tattered remains of the few inadequate legal workplace protections American employees still have.

Who are the enemies of the working public? Its employers. In 1996, large corporations who spent 19 times labor's $60 million on campaign contributions. They got what they paid for. The subcommittees of the House Committee on Education and the Workforce, began disassembling the EEOC and OSHA to get government off the backs of employers.

The death of federal worker protections is imminent. These scorched earth initiatives are done on behalf of the "new" worker who needs to move freely among employers selling his talents to the highest bidder, as a free agent does in professional sports.

Of course, the question about why there must be movement in the first place goes begging. This line of reasoning suggests that historical job security is imprisoning for workers who "deserve" to start anew every couple of years.

In every town, the local Chamber of Commerce, heavily populated by realtors and builders, acts as the unelected leadership who brings urban sprawl and traffic. Chamber membership is often the springboard to name recognition and electability.

The Chamber portrays itself as a benign good citizen, making highly visible contributions to local organizations and contributing to local causes. But beneath this cover of community service, beats a callous anti-employee heart. One formal 1998 initiative and one representative court action tell the true story about Chamber values.

The U.S. Chamber of Commerce blames employees for "frivolous" lawsuits against employers that prove costly to Chamber members. So, in 1998 the Chamber launched an attack on employees' rights to sue employers.

Since most Chamber members are small businesses, traditionally exempt from most state and federal regulations, employees who are mistreated or terminated seeking a remedy have only the court system. Going to court requires a lawyer.

In 1998, the US Chamber declared war on the Association of Trial Lawyers of America (ATLA) whose members represent employee-plaintiffs accusing defendant employers of harassment, defamation, abuse, discrimination and wrongful termination. Never mind that only a fraction of complaints ever turn into lawsuits. Additionally, fewer than half of all employee-initiated lawsuits make it to trial. And the whining employers win 75.5% of the trial decisions. How dare they cry foul!

The war is a lobbying war between the ATLA and the U.S. Chamber of Commerce in state legislatures. It is about dueling trade association fundraising to pay lobbyists, their conduit to influence over elected officials. Make no mistake, the Chamber embarked on an anti-employee campaign. It called upon 200,000 members to pony up the bucks to fuel the distortion campaign.

Larry Kraus, a Chamber senior VP, believes that 75% of lawsuits faced by Chamber members involve charges of bias by employees. So, conditions for filing a suit will be curtailed in this drive for so-called "tort reform." In addition, the Chamber is pushing for "loser pays" legislation. The loser in a civil action would have to pay the legal bills for both sides. This slap action is sure to discourage already tormented employees from exercising their only means of seeking redress from a bullying employer.

Legal action is portrayed as "frivolous" when an employee sues. In mid-February 1998, a federal appellate court granted the delay of an OSHA initiative as requested by the U.S. Chamber of Commerce!

The Chamber hopes to prevent employees from using the courts. Through legal action, OSHA was stopped from giving the 12,250 worst workplace safety offending employers an incentive to reduce the likelihood of safety and health inspections. Targeted companies faced a certain annual inspection because of their documented failure to protect employee safety, but OSHA had a plan.

OSHA had tested and perfected a program for employers that was proven to reduce workplace injuries and illnesses. The underfunded, frequently attacked safety watchdog agency prom-ised to the most dangerous companies that adopted the safety program a reduction of inspections from 100% to 30%. That was promoted as getting government off their backs.

In court, the Chamber called the incentive plan "coercive" to its members who ignored the federal mandate and the moral obligation to provide a safe workplace for employees. The court agreed to suspend OSHA's ability to give the dangerous compa-nies a choice.

The Chamber is not the employee's friend. Its claim of com-munity service at the local level is hypocritical. Lest we forget, the community is comprised of employees. Employees are the target of the Chamber's assault on civil rights and safety in workplaces owned by Chamber members.

Lawyers for Employees Only

If you are the target of harassment from a bully, in most situations, the bully will not have broken the law. This accounts for much of the frustration about workplace bullying.

Federal laws dictate under what limited circumstances you are protected. We are not lawyers and cannot interpret the law for you. The National Employee Rights Institute published *Job Rights and Survival Strategies* by attorneys Paul Tobias and Susan Sauter. The following brief summary of the anti-discrimi-nation acts was adapted from that book.

Title VII of the Civil Rights Act protects employees from discrimination if they are members of one of the "protected classes:" according to race, color, religion, national origin or sex (including discrimination based on pregnancy).

Employees are protected from age discrimination under the Age Discrimination in Employment Act (ADEA) for workers age 40 years or older. However, beginning in 1997, the courts have begun to allow employers to claim "economic reasons" to cut

loose older workers who just happen to earn the higher salaries, thus eroding federal safeguards.

It is also against federal law to discriminate based on disability (defined as a physical or mental condition that substan-
tially limits a person in a major life function or functions). Only
permanent, chronic or long-term conditions apply, according to
the Americans With Disabilities Act (ADA).

In nearly every other instance of workplace bullying,
whether or not your complaint has legal merit will depend on
the ingenuity of the legal counsel you hire We recommend calling the National Employment Lawyers Association (NELA) national office (415-227-4655) for a recommendation to an employment attorney in your area. Remember, you want a labor
or plaintiff-only attorney. Plaintiffs are employees who complain
against employers, abusing individuals or unions. Attorneys who
represent both sides may have a conflict of interest as well as
hidden biases that could affect your case.

As we said, we are frustrated with lawyers. We're not sure
whether to blame them for their helplessness or to fault the
steady erosion of employee protection laws by heavily-financed
corporate interests.

The U.S. Chamber of Commerce has also declared war on
trial attorneys who represent employees vowing to fight an
employee's right to bring cases against employers. The Chamber wants to chill lawsuits, and they will accomplish this by
requiring that the loser in court pays legal fees of the winner.

So, lawyers who represent plaintiffs are the good guys, but
they are rarely the crusader atop the white steed that you might
imagine or wish for. Ideally, they want fees paid up front, a
retainer. However, contingency contracts are more common (up
to 40% of damages won plus expenses) if they believe you will
win damages from a civil suit.

Attorneys with expertise in Employment law, unless they
are NELA members or restrict their practices to plaintiffs, probably represent both employers and employees. Which type of

client do you think brings in the greater revenue to attorneys? Employers come second. The attorney is obligated to tell you if she or he has a conflict of interest in your particular case. A partner in the same firm might represent the employer in other cases. When this happens, the attorney should disqualify her- or himself.

The Work Doctor's Lawyer Interview

Here's The Work Doctor's condensed guide to what to look for when selecting an employment lawyer. Ask questions if the attorney does not offer this information during the initial telephone call.

- a fighting spirit
- an ability to be empathetic, to share outrage at your plight
- wisdom based on direct experience in court
- a stable of satisfied clients (ask for telephone numbers)
- experience with similar cases brought against similar defendants
- memory for the details of your case (ask former clients)
- how and when will you be prepared for your appearance at a deposition
- who is assigned to be your primary contact person?
- frequency of regular case updates
- a caseload that allows time for attention to your case
- reputation within local employment lawyer community
- results:
  - overall percentage of claims settled (at what stage)

- percentage of cases gone to trial
- victory percentage
- average monetary award won for clients
- willingness to accept case on contingency (court costs paid by firm or by you) vs. retainer and fees as you go

Our simple reminder to you is that if you must engage an attorney, you will still have to carry the majority of the burden for winning your case. You, and only you, will provide much of the information and be the steadiest source of new angles and approaches they could take when they get discouraged. And if you expect them to prop you up emotionally, forget it. You must have a support network in place to help you keep your balance.

The Courts

The least helpful people on your side are the courts—judges and juries. Do not believe employer groups who warn their members that frivolous lawsuits brought by disgruntled employees will put owners out of business.

According to this type of disinformation propaganda, cases that bottleneck the courts are filed by fun-loving employees who suffered nothing more than irreparable "personality conflicts" with benevolent, but misunderstood, bosses. This is pure fiction, a mythology that unites business owners and large employers against employees.

Here are some facts that should buoy employer confidence in the court system. At the same time, it should scare the hell out of an employee like you who deserves legal redress for suffering at the hands of a workplace bully.

- There's been a steady decline in the number of class action suits against employers filed by the EEOC (the federal agency responsible for ensuring that the federal protected classes of employees are not discriminated against). In 1976, 1174 suits were filed. The anemic, understaffed EEOC had only 68 class-action cases active in 1996.

- How about those costly accommodations for the disabled? The ADA was supposed to drive many large companies out of business. On the contrary, it was found that Sears spent an average of only $45 per person in direct costs to adjust the workplace to meet the needs of 71 workers. Not a budget buster, if done wisely!

- Sexual harassment is not the plague employers portray it to be. A recent study by the University of Illinois found that despite huge efforts by women's groups to educate the public, few women who are harassed, according to the legal definition, recognize it when it's done to them. So, in fact, fewer report it and fewer still file a claim.

- The median jury award in a sexual harassment case is $100,500. The median award granted to those who claimed job discrimination in federal court was $100,000 in 1994, a trend in decline.

- The number of people who actually file a claim with the EEOC for discrimination of any kind is less than 6 in 10,000 employees.

- The 1991 Civil Rights Act made possible both jury trials and punitive damages for discrimination cases. For the dozen years prior to the Act, just 24% of the cases went to a jury. Employees (plaintiffs) won 24% of the time. Between 1991 and

1995, the employee win rate creeped to 30% despite a doubling of the percentage of cases heard by juries. Still, less than half the cases ever go to a jury!

Do the math. Employees 30, Employers 70. Who wins? Employers have no right to whine. A most unsettling comparison is made by Theodore Eisenberg, a Cornell University law professor stating that "job discrimination cases remain one of the single most unsuccessful classes of litigation for plaintiffs. They settle less and lose more than almost anything else." The only class of complaints with a lower success rate is the one filed by prisoners who mostly represent themselves.

• Pre-trial settlements are not typically expensive for employers. True, the amounts paid by Texaco ($176 million), Publix Markets ($80 million), Home Depot ($80+ million) grab headlines and fuel employer apprehension. The statistical reality is much different. A methodical analysis of wrongful termination cases in California courts during a recent 7 year period resulted in the following: 17% were dropped, costing employers on the average of less than $500, 40% were settled before a trial costing an average of $60,000 including attorneys' fees.

• As always, headlines are deceiving. Dramatic awards like $50 million to a single WalMart employee are often drastically reduced on appeal. $50 million became $385,000. Judges often set aside jury generosity.

Carla was fresh out of graduate school and eager to launch a research career. She won a low-paying position at the massive, presitigous state university working for a scholar with an international reputation in her field. Carla loved research more than teaching; it was her calling. She planned on a decades-long career collecting data, authoring journal articles, writing books, giving symposia, the flurry of activities that announced that this academic had made a mark in her field.

Then on one project the highly esteemed scholar-boss asked Carla for her shoebox of raw data. Not thinking twice, she handed it over. There was some talk of publishing articles based on the data, but Carla began to feel left out of activities. The boss refused to return Carla's data when asked. When the scholar-boss' boss was told about the theft, he threatened to fire Carla if she continued to complain. She did and he fired her. For four years, Carla was without a full-time academic job to replace the one stolen from her. She taught courses on campus on a part-time basis, while simultaneously pleading with university administration to retrieve her data and give her job back.

At the end of the fifth year, she finally took the two supervising professors—the thief and the hatchet man—to court. A jury found them guilty of theft and illegal retaliation (see what can be done when a lawyer can see possibilities beyond the narrow scope of the law against discrimination). The initial jury award for damages was over $1.5 million. The university legal eagles dug in and appealed. It took a total of 10 years from the date of the original bullying acts before the case ran its course through the appeals process. The university never gave up, nor did it ever acknowledge blame. The thief and hatchet man still work there. Carla has completely given up on the academe. She's goin' to law school!

Dilbert® As Proxy

Everyone knows the widely popular comic strip about the cubicle world that passes for the world of work. Scott Adams, the creator, populates the strip with idiot bosses, idiot co-workers, and names of the latest management fads foisted on unsuspecting workers.

The reason for including a comic strip in the list of helpers is because so many workers have made Adams their employee advocate. Many people too timid to directly confront those who hurt them simply clip the cartoon and pass it anonymously under the door of the boss or bully. They want the strip to speak for them.

This communication ritual goes both ways. Bosses feel as comfortable using the ersatz method of relating to workers as they do being the recipient. It's a silent substitute for tackling the causes of the problems everyone snickers about. What bothers us at Campaign headquarters is that silence is the bully's friend.

As a bullied employee, you should be concerned that Adams, an MBA and former mid-level manager, is not the employees' friend, an illusory image the public seems to want to bestow on him. To the *Washingon Post,* he declared "I never had any integrity. This was always meant to be a business." In an interview in a 1997 interview *with Editor & Publisher,* Adams stated, "Actually, my only intention is for people to transfer their money to me."

The only book critical of the snowballing mass media merchandising empire that is Dilbert is *The Trouble With Dilbert* by Norman Solomon. The book takes the comic strip's popularity as proof that employees recognize that the way corporations operate has to change (we assume this would include stopping bullies). The tragedy, according to Solomon, is that fans of the cartoon strip vent their anger and symbolically thumb their nose at the boss or employee without taking any risky action that could improve an unsatisfactory workplace.

We feel good laughing at a comic strip. Let's not forget that it is also important to confront the real demons that plague your life. No book of funnies is a good substitute for you acting as your own advocate.

Your Best Advocate Is You

Let institutionalized helpers help, but be aware of their limitations. Optimize their usefulness to you by knowing their shortcomings. For most of us, we have to weigh carefully the decision to rely on institutionalized helpers for anything.

Engaging co-workers can be helpful for your bully busting campaign. Right now, they either can't or won't help.

Confronting your bully is the least expensive—in terms of money and emotion—and quickest way to regain personal dignity. Your fate is best managed when in your hands.

Section Two
Stop The Hurt

*Originality and the feeling of one's own dignity
are achieved only through work and struggle.
- Fyodor Dostoyevsky*

Chapter 7
Assessing the Bully's Impact

*You have to take it as it happens, but you should try
to make it happen the way you want to take it.*
- German proverb

Chapter preview:
Cycles of self-confidence
Assessing impact before it's too late
Interpret the impact table
Changing your perspective

Cycles of Self-Confidence

When exposed to a bully, most people go through 3 stages of emotions.

1. the pre-bully, positive-about-your-job stage

2. then the bullying starts and you bend over back-wards to please the bully without success

3. finally, you can no longer ignore your frustrations and you explode at the bully, leaving you feeling even more terrible than before

The phases go something like this. You get a new job and you are eager to go to work. You are ready to do all you can do, not only for yourself, but for your boss and your company. You come to work ready to move mountains. No task is impossible.

Usually, this over-enthusiasm fades within the first month, and you settle down to producing the best work you can.

Then, you become aware something is wrong. You don't seem to be able to do anything right. Your good ideas are not recognized. Soon you are questioning whether or not you have the capability to do your work at all. The more you try and improve, the more your boss or co-worker gets angry at you.

You have run into a bully. Instead of questioning the truth or logic of the bully's antics, you imagine that you are not doing something you should do. You then decide you must change in some way. But, regardless of any change you make, the bully still continues to find fault with you or your work. This, in turn, makes you even more determined to find a way to please the bully who will never be pleased.

When you have exhausted every avenue (and then some) and you still are not doing it right, you become frustrated. You have done everything to please, why can't the bully understand? Why can't she see how hard you are trying? Why isn't your best effort good enough?

Then comes the explosion. One day when you have been harassed and shamed beyond your limit, you explode. You look the bully straight in the eye and you say, "leave me alone." "I'm doing the best I can." "Just leave me alone."

Your explosion does not make you feel better, it only makes you feel worse. You begin to think, "What if she were right? What if my work is inferior?" Now you've really done it, you've alienated the one person you need to keep your job.

Sound familiar? That is the reaction most people have when they are faced with continuous bullying. You feel your best just isn't good enough. You are full of self-doubt.

Finally, you begin to see the pattern in this sick cycle. You question why this is happening. You decide it is really not you. Now it is time to stop the bully, once and for all.

Getting to the step at which you know it's time to stop the noise, the lies, the venom from the bully is made more complicated because you are immersed in hurt. It's easy to lose track of how deep your troubles are.

> *A scientist heated a pan of water to a high temperature. Then, she tried to put a live frog into it. The frog jumped out immediately. A second frog was put in a pan of cold water that was gradually heated to boiling. That frog never tried to jump. It was boiled to death.*
>
> *- A parable*

Adaptation to a fatal environment carries a price. Only much later, sometimes too late, do people realize the price they have paid for going along with someone else's hurtful plan for their future.

It's important to assess the bully's impact before it's too late.

Assessing Impact Before It's Too Late

We present two exercises to help you when the bully attempts to control. It is important that **you** control the definitions of who you are.

For *each* exercise, A and B, there *are two sets of questions* to ask.

Exercise A

You have seen how to recognize bullying. The first exercise is designed to help you counter the bully's false accusations so you can remind yourself of just how competent you are.

There are four areas that will help you begin your recovery from bullying. There are four areas or aspects about yourself that you, friends, family and co-workers (if any can be trusted) will evaluate.

The four areas are:

How I Relate To Others

Descriptions of strengths and weaknesses in relationships with friends and co-workers

How Other People See Me

Do you get along well with others? Are you seen as angry? Helpful to others? Shy?

My Performance at Work

Describe the way you handle job assignments, are you on time? A procastinator? A "neatnick"?

My Ability To Reason and Solve Problems

Do you like the freedom to improvise? A quick learner? Special knowledge in certain areas?

Now take some time to write down as many phrases as you can on the following page to describe yourself. Be candid with yourself. Don't be shy or humble.

Note: As with all exercises, we suggest that you create lists and fill in boxes on separate pages so that parts of this book may be shared with friends without the risk of revealing information you'd prefer to keep to yourself.

How I Relate to Others:

How Other People See Me:

My Performance At Work:

My Ability To Solve Problems:

Now make two blank copies of the series of questions. Give one to a trusted friend or co-worker, and one to a supportive family member. Ask them to jot down how they feel you do in each of the four areas (these are to be shared only with you).

When the sheets are returned, lay them side-by-side. Do you see similarities? What are your strengths. Do you judge yourself too harshly?

Exercise B

This exercise is another way to evaluate how BullyProof you are in the following three areas. Add any dimensions or aspects that are important to you.

Quality of Relationships With Others

This is an indirect indicator of whether or not the bully has poisoned the good relationships you have with others. First, evaluate how you see the Quality with family and friends. Then, have family members rate the relationship they each have with you. Repeat for friends (as before, co-workers may be included, if they are trustworthy). The pattern that emerges can send a warning signal of pending trouble.

We have noticed that many couples are severely strained when one person is bullied. Split-ups and divorces are common. The worst-case scenario is when the bullied Target loses track of the decline in quality and the partner waits too long to tell her how he is impacted.

Confidence in Personal Competence

This area taps resilience under duress, the ability to focus on "the work" in a storm, and the firmness of your belief in yourself as being right and not deserving the mistreatment received. All bullies, regardless of the particular tactics used, aim to erode the Target's belief in herself. The erosion of this confidence is perhaps the most devastating effect bullies can have. It is among the toughest setbacks from which Targets have to recover.

Emotional Effectiveness

Bullies play on Targets' emotions heavily in order to push them out of control. Too much or too little emotion can be problematic. Make a special note to see who among the list of evaluators believes that you have no right to be hurt or mad.

Of course, you should add any aspects of your life that the bully has tried to dominate to this short list. Then, complete the 4-step process described on the following pages for each aspect or dimension.

First set of questions

Turn a critical eye toward yourself. As honestly as you can, state what you *Do Well* and what you *Could Do Better* in a 2-column table like the one below. Record observations about yourself, as you see yourself. Answer the question for yourself, strictly from your personal point of view.

After you fill in your answers, you can compare both the quantity and quality of responses. You are not necessarily immune from the bully's attempts to control and influence you just because the list under *Do Well* is longer than under *Could Do Better.* Only you can know if the items in one column are more important than items in the other.

Example

Let's demonstrate how the exercise works for the first worklife area--Quality of Relationships With Others. You will rate that quality, as you define it, strictly *from your point of view.* If the good news (*Do Well*) outweighs the bad (*Could Do Better*), then it's safe to say that you feel Relationships With Others have remained relatively immune from damage.

QUALITY OF MY RELATIONSHIPS WITH . . .

	Do Well	*Could Do Better*
Rating Myself		

Second set of questions

Ask trustworthy friends and family to rate, *in their opinion,* your contribution to the Quality of the Relationship they have with you. In other words, you will ask them to say what you *Do Well* and how you *Could Do Better,* strictly from *their point of view.* Each person answers for her- or himself only.

QUALITY OF YOUR RELATIONSHIP WITH ME

	Do Well	*Could Do Better*
Friends		
Family		

RATERS

There's no need for raters to see the comments of others. Encourage brutal frankness. This tool works only if raters are honest and forthcoming. When raters are truthful, you will discover problems that you did not, nor could not, see for yourself.

On the other hand, if raters prefer to tell you what they think *you* want to hear (and minimize the bad news), you and they might stay in denial. Without candor, no changes are possible.

Next, assemble an Impact Table summarizing the observations that you and the others noted.

QUALITY OF RELATIONSHIPS

	Do Well	*Could Do Better*
Self		
Friends		
Family		

RATERS

Interpret The Impact Table

Make the comparisons between columns of opinions that others provided. Compare the rows. Look for patterns.

Who thinks you are relatively BullyProof?

Regarding what aspects?

In what areas are you blind, and therefore, vulnerable?

Who sees the effects of the bullying experience as you do?

Are they right or are those who disagree with you right?

How are the differences in observations related to the different levels of support you receive?

On whom can you count for a reality check when needed?

Have you lost your sense of perspective?

Are you the frog in boiling water?

Repeat this 4-step process for each relevant aspect of your worklife.

1. Do your self-rating
2. Ask others to rate you
3. Summarize the observations in an Impact Table
4. Interpret patterns for meaning. Regain perspective

CONFIDENCE IN PERSONAL COMPETENCE

	Do Well	*Could Do Better*
Self		
Friends		
Family		

RATERS

EMOTIONAL EFFECTIVENESS

	Do Well	*Could Do Better*
Self		
Friends		
Family		

RATERS

Changing Your Perspective

After you have decided what things you can do to change the way you act and feel at work, there is a simple tool to help you when you encounter bullying behaviors.

The way you look at situations with the bully will dramatically affect your attitude. Practice dissociating yourself from unpleasant memories. By mentally stepping away from an unpleasant event or a bully, you can adjust your point of view. Remember, you can never change the behaviors of the bully, you can only make changes in yourself.

Try using the following three steps to re-evaluate your situation with a bully.

Step 1.

Compare your bully problems to a catastrophic event? Does this compare to losing a leg or a loved one? Do you need a different perspective on this situation?

Step 2.

Mentally edit the memory of your encounter with the bully as if you were editing a film. As you replay your last encounter, view it as if came from another camera angle. Turn the camera so you can try look at it in different ways. Go over the memory with a friend to try and get a new perspective on the situation.

Step 3.

Reframe the problem and change the meaning of the experience. Try to look at the experience as a positive event rather than an attack on you. Are there any ways the bullying experience could be positive?

Chapter 8
Establishing and Protecting Boundaries

No one can make you feel inferior
without your consent.
                    - Eleanor Roosevelt

Boundaries are central to separating who you are from who the bully wants you to believe you are. Much of what applies to understanding boundaries, carries over into other areas that also trip up Targets.

Much of a person's identity and self-confidence comes from having appropriate boundaries in place for protection against assaults by bullies who seek only to control and hurt you.

Two boundary characteristics that affect, and are affected by bullying, are:

- your personally chosen and defined boundaries, established so you can live your life the way you seek and want, and
- your boundaries' susceptibility to invasion by a bully.

Boundaries Defined

In its simplest definition, a boundary is an unseen, unmeasurable limit or barrier that simultaneously creates an inside and an outside. It is an invisible wall with two sides.

Inside each individual boundary resides an identity—personal, family or group. Challenges to those identities are launched by invading bullies from the outside who want to dictate the terms of a Target's identity.

For our purposes here, we speak of psychological boundaries. They can be identified by gauging your tolerance for having them invaded. Invasions of personal boundaries by others causes discomfort, an anxiety. When uncomfortable enough, we typically take steps to stop the invader that caused the pain.

People have different thresholds. Some have a higher tolerance for letting others meddle in their lives; some tolerate little to no meddling. Meddling ranges from suggestions about how you should live your life (typically tolerated from close friends) to full-scale verbal assaults by bullies, repeatedly telling you how incompetent and worthless you are.

The greatest danger a Target faces in the work-world is to have loose or non-existent boundaries. That person becomes an unprotected Target for all who love to hurt others.

One way to repel invasions by bullies is to use verbal commands to stop the bullying behavior, to announce that a line has been crossed, that you have a policy of zero tolerance for such unacceptable actions and that it will be enforced. This is "tit for tat." Most bullies invade Targets with words. Most Targets have little experience dealing with verbal assaults.

INVASION → DISCOMFORT → REPEL INVASION

Below are categories of boundaries. This list starts at the primary boundary of personal identity and widens to include one's social world.

Identity Boundaries
   • Physical/Personal Space
   • Emotions
   • The Self
Family Boundaries
   • Unit Solidarity
   • Empathy
   • Work-Leisure & Family
Work/Social Boundaries
   • Jobs
   • Friends, Co-Workers, Supporters

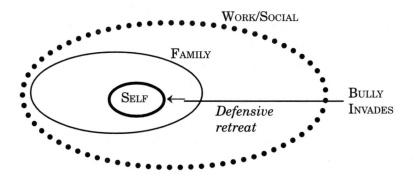

Depiction of a bully invasion piercing protective boundaries in stages, with the Self serving as the Target's last stand.

Identity Boundaries

Skin, Touch & Space

The knowledge of separateness from the world begins in the crib. Just connecting the act of swinging your little baby foot with moving the mobile begins the journey to Selfhood. Your developing infant brain gets and implants the message that you are *not* your environment. Though your mind cannot yet fathom philosophy, you know that there is an "out there." Miraculously, you've taken the first step toward an "internal you." The assembly of a consciousness begins that early.

For humans, our skin literally becomes the physical boundary between us and the external world. It is through that skin that so much brain and neural development takes place. Touch stimulates and comforts. It is the language of love, nurturance and acceptance. The absence of touch sets the stage for needy, love-starved adults.

The rules about who you allow to touch your skin develop in childhood. Nearly everyone touches an infant.

As you grow older, based on cultural mores and family tradition, strangers will be forbidden to share the intimate zone of touching skin. When the unwritten rule about touching is violated, you automatically get anxious and take evasive action. That's why inappropriate contact by strangers is a hostile gesture.

Emotions

Emotions are also learned in childhood and follow family- and peer-specific unwritten norms, rules. Learned early in life are:
- expressivity: how emotions are publicly displayed, and
- labeling: names given to internal feelings in response to events.

There are entire textbooks written about the healthy development of human emotions. Growing up with very few inhibitions about expressing feelings tends to create adults who readily show their feelings. It's good to grow up free from much of the anxiety that seems to burden those who live scripted lives. An uninhibited spirit is less likely to suffer from stress.

☞ The point most relevant to workplace bullying is that people who naturally show emotions will generally be seen as more vulnerable than those with a closed style.

In the American workplace, enthusiastic people jeopardize the illusion of cool (emotionless) rationality that many others believe should characterize work. Detachment (a glazed-over non-responsiveness to their world, according to some) is a key ingredient in "professionalism."

You have the right to call your emotions what you want. Gut feelings are ambiguous. They are normal reactions to potential stressors in your life. The emotional label you choose determines whether the feeling is positive or negative.

The impact of feelings

Imagine the gut-wrenching, sweaty-palms feeling as you're about to turn in a project you've worked on for 6 months. If the person you're giving it to is the office tyrant, your sworn enemy, you're likely to call that swirling feeling nausea in anticipation of the undeserved verbal tirade you've come to expect. You're literally sick, knowing that she will bark about how "stupid and incompetent" you are. You condition yourself to recognize the symptoms as those of impending shame. No one should have the right to inflict shame on you or be able to trigger it through fearful anticipation!

On the other hand, if you're submitting the project to the person who promised a promotion and raise when it was done, those are harmless butterflies in anticipation of a new phase of your career. You're dizzy with the anticipation of spending the extra money and all the recognition a new job brings with it.

Same stomach, different names for the feeling that goes with physiological symptoms. Research has shown that we're all somewhat susceptible to labeling of our emotions by others when the feelings are unclear. However, it's dangerous when you are ready to experience a positive emotion and an outsider barges in and defines the feeling for you. In anxious times, we are more susceptible to an invasion of our emotional boundaries.

The Self - Putting It All Together

All the "firsts" in our life begin in early infancy with parental relationships. Besides meeting our needs for food and shelter, parents set the stage for developing either strong or weak selves. When old enough to interact with others besides parents, the Self is further developed by peers who shape you into what you are and will become. Nevertheless, the final product called "you" continues to develop through a lifetime. The core—your fundamental approach to how you deal with what life throws you—is predominantly determined at a young age.

With a well-developed Self in place, you can resist all attempts by others to define your identity, to invade your personal space without permission, and to define feelings for you. A poorly developed Self seems to doom adults to search outside themselves for answers to inner questions. This renders them more vulnerable to influence by others. It is not a question of goodness or badness, rather a matter of dependency on others for definitions. Bullies consume dependent people.

The Self is the safe place to which you can retreat when under attack. It is the one boundary that should never be compromised, invaded or traded away to get along with another person. Think of it as the innermost circle inside several other concentric circles. You and you alone control access to it. And the re-programming of the lifetime of scripts stored there will be undertaken only by you, on your terms. Any changes are yours alone to make.

☞ Let's not get bogged down in psychobabble here. Simply put, never discount the importance of selfhood. All feelings of adult worthiness, entitlement to certain "rights," pride and competence flow from experiences many of which were too early to recall.

Family Boundaries

Family-of-Origin Factors

Our first social group is our family-of-origin, a group of manageable size. The Family-of-Origin is the place to rehearse behaviors for the larger world of strangers in which we don't always get our way. Families teach us to be social beings, capable of respecting or disregarding others. In a healthy family, a child is taught to develop a self-concept separate and different from other family members.

Healthy families also provide unconditional support for us as blossoming little people. Ideally, parents and older siblings foster independence by teaching us to fend for ourselves, while tolerating dependence on the family for comfort in the toughest of times.

Family Interactions and Targethood

Unfortunately, there are families that live with sick "enmeshed patterns," better described as smothering rather than helpful. One for all and all for one sounds like teamwork until the identities of all the children and usually one parent are sacrificed. Distinct personalities rarely emerge from such families. Enmeshed families squash the human need to become an individual, to matter, to be special in some unique way.

"Disengaged" families are equally defeating. They are families where members have little contact with each other. There is little to no love. Children grow up believing they are worthless, needing to justify in their own minds the neglect they experience.

Adults who grew up with either of these disturbed arrangements are likely to rely too heavily on people at work for support, validation and even for an identity. Bullies smell neediness and exploit it to their advantage.

Healthy Families

Healthy families form a protective boundary behind which adults and children can retreat to safety when and if necessary. It's a much looser boundary, woven more by solidarity among family members, than the shell around the Self.

A bully is a person who denies her emotions (low expressivity). She operates from rigid boundaries. In her disengaged Family-of-Origin, she was not connected with her parents. Because of this, her feelings were not developed or brought to the surface. More importantly, when any feelings do surface for her, she easily becomes overwhelmed and withdraws from all contact with others.

Empathy

Another gift taught in healthy families is empathy. Empathy is the human capacity to understand, intellectually, what another person is going through when things go poorly and to recognize the emotional state of that person because you've gone through it. Sympathy is cold; that's why pity serves no purpose. Empathy is sympathy with emotions included. It is the basis of compassion. Families are the first teachers of compassion.

Empathy requires the loosening of rigid, personal protective boundaries. It involves letting in the experiences of others. Empathy is always considered one of humankind's higher level traits. Unfortunately, the openness and compassion that characterize empathy render you vulnerable to assaults from a bully who despises positive traits. As a witness to the bullying of another person, it is empathy that will compel you to take action to alleviate the Target's suffering.

☞ In general, bullies are thwarted by independent Targets and don't bother with them. Research in workplace aggression found that bullies are essentially lazy. They prefer easier-to-control, vulnerable Targets.

Work / Family

When you're the adult and parent, you face the issues of allocating your energy and time across family and work activities. The critical boundary question is how much intrusion by work into your private time will be tolerated. The answer is necessarily personal. Some advisers sketch pie charts slicing an ideal life into several domains: income-generating, physical health, learning, love and spiritual slices, to name a few. Their concern is balance.

☞ For BullyProofing yourself, the concern is whether or not you can fight work's intrusive effect on the rest of your life. Targets under fire from bullies may try to keep the torment a secret from everyone at home. However, the strain takes its toll in small, unavoidable ways. There may be loss of sleep, increased moodiness, a shorter fuse for getting angry, and general depression. Astute family members cannot help but notice, but may say nothing until you, the Target, share the cause of your grief or ask for help.

The thing to remember during bullying is that the family is affected. Families cannot help but be disturbed by trouble at work. Trying to will away the negative impact of bullying on the family with words ("I won't discuss at home what happens in that hellhole") or the shutting down of discussion about it during family time prevents Targets from getting the support and love they so desperately need to offset the lies and isolation of work. Also, the family, as a unit, can brainstorm together what can be done to bust the bully, to turn off the source of the pain. Attempting to go it alone while feigning a calm, collected exterior is foolhardy.

Well-intentioned Targets want to spare their families the hurt, but that wastes too much time and energy. It's better to recruit the family's help right from the start. Isolated Targets are weakened. Targets backed bya family's love can shorten the period of vulnerability. Supported Targets can move forward quicker and re-establish a normal work-family barrier when work is again more normal.

Work/Social Boundaries

A word first to relate social to identity boundaries. Social boundaries are looser and less permanent because so many people share in their development and maintenance. Nothing is as personal, nor should be as inviolate, as a person's identity.

The Job

Based on the figure depicting family and personal boundaries embedded within the work/social boundary, you can see how far from a personal identity the job should lie.

That is, your identity was formed long ago and is very distinct from what you do for a living. At least that's true for the majority of folks. There are few among us whose work and soul are deliberately fused and inseparable (usually artists).

For the rest of us mere mortals, and nearly everyone who gets bullied, it is critical to separate your identity from the job. Jobs are frequently snatched away without warning, without care for the consequences facing you and your family. If every time you change jobs, you had to change the person you are, you'd be exhausted from the task of restructuring a life several times (5-7 changes, according to recent surveys).

Jobs pass and are shared by hundreds, if not thousands, of others. Your identity has to remain relatively permanent to lend stability and purpose to your life. When you can no longer count on a job, you still must be able to count on the uniqueness that is you.

> ☞ Here is the critical point about job boundaries. Assaults on boundaries force the Target into a defensive position. The question you have to ask yourself is whether or not a job is worth defending ("I have to have this job, there are no others for me," "I can't do anything else," "I have to hold onto this job that tortures me daily because it's easier to get a job when you have a job."). It's especially painful to hear advice seekers defend holding onto a job (thus showing a strong job boundary) while describing the incredible destruction bullying has brought to their lives.

With this logic, Targets elevate the importance of keeping a specific job at the expense of their self-worth as if they deserve no better. They have allowed an invasion of their identity boundary. This rationalization and compromise appears costly. The key to survival is for Targets to know that there will be another job. If the current job with the bully kills them, they won't have to work.

Friends, Co-Workers, Supporters

This boundary captures the widest group of non-related people in your world. It is not of a uniform size, thickness or permeability. It is in a constant state of flux.

Essentially, this boundary separates those in your "in-group" from those not within your inner circle, the "out-group." In broad societal terms, common grouping variables include profession, religion, race, age, gender and special interests. These are broad group identities that may be invoked when you and your peers gather together for breaks and social events.

The co-worker boundary is a good example of how a temporary, constantly changing group identity can hurt Targets of bullying. One day, the group is commiserating about the bully's torment. They may even share stories of misery while they themselves were the bully's Targets. As a reasonable person, you might assume that all co-workers will stand together to fight the bully in front of the boss.

However, the next day you, the Target, may suddenly and inexplicably find yourself out of the group and left to fend for yourself. You stand alone with your plight. It is as if the frank gripe sessions never happened. The many reasons for this turn-around are based on fear.

The feelings of abandonment by a group that originally supported you compounds the pain inflicted by the bully. They become unwitting accomplices. When a group turns on you and isolates you, it is easy to doubt that you are right and the bully is wrong. The speed with which a group forms, disbands, and re-forms should send a warning that groups deserve the least trust.

Unions are also a group to which you may belong, whose ostensible purpose is to defend your rights. However, they, too are prone to abandon you for various reasons driven by the group's survival priorities rather than the merits of your case. They satisfy their contractual obligation by starting the grievance process, but that is long, tortuous and inefficient for dealing with daily bullying. The courage of a special individual in the group willing to take risks on your behalf is more important than any group identity.

Boundaries and Defenses

When facing assaults from a bully and retreating to a defensive position, it's natural to first seek validation from your work group for the perception that you're not crazy. If it's a team of turncoats, you will get no support. The response to this rejection is to focus entirely on your job. Targets try to "stick to the job" and ignore all the madness manufactured by the bully, thus, going it alone at work.

Then, when intense concentration to your job fails to serve as a distraction from bullying, the next possible source of comfort is the family. Sadly, even families can tire of the steady stream of workplace horror stories. We wish it were not true, but it is a rare family that gives unconditional support from the beginning to the absolute end of a bully's campaign.

This leaves the final source of comfort to be the Self. It's the circle within the circles, the innermost one, the one sure thing you have to be able to count on—faith in your identity.

Of course, this model of levels or layers of boundaries that one after another fail to ward off the bully is the worst case scenario. In the best of all possible worlds (though rarely occurring), your work group stands solidly with you so that you have multiple sources of support with family and identity providing additional support. With all boundaries intact, a bully has no chance to overcome a Target.

Boundary Rights

Cats and dogs

The writer Mary Bly, compares boundaries with cats and dogs. "Dogs," she writes, "come when they are called; cats take a message and get back to you."

Dogs always want to be close to people. They will jump on our laps (no matter what their size), or come on the bed, always trying to get as close as possible. Their boundaries are very close and they expect all other animals to have the same boundaries.

Cats, on the other hand, have very distinct boundaries. They come and go when they want and if they want. Even when they want to be close, they determine when and how and where. They are aware of the humans in the room, but human movements do not interrupt what they are doing. Their boundaries are very different from dogs. Cats need more space and their boundaries are more rigid.

Like cats and dogs we all grow up with different boundaries. We learn and tend to practice the boundaries we were taught as children. We tend to see them in black and white and rarely even question them. What we fail to see is that boundaries are not only black and white, but also come in shades of gray.

Avoiding Spineless Flexibility

The contrast to rigid boundaries is when boundaries are so flexible that they can't hold shape. When you encounter someone with loose boundaries you will see that they are like chameleons.

Lisa is a chameleon. At work she will agree with a co-worker that their boss is unreasonable. Ten minutes later when someone else states that she feels their boss is a great and under-

standing fellow, Lisa will agree with her. She is unable to let the phone ring at lunch or at the end of the day for fear she will miss something important and get into trouble. Thus, she misses many lunches and spends hours working after 5 pm, just to finish the work that was interrupted by phone calls.

Because Lisa's boundaries are too flexible she often feels overwhelmed with life and work. Each new demand distracts her. She has difficulty setting priorities and following them. She gets started on one task only to get sidetracked by something else. She may appear disorganized.

Maintaining Your Boundaries in the Face of Power

Certain roles carry rank or power. Parent, supervisor, boss, teacher, coach, doctor, policeman are examples of roles that carry power. It is important, however, to know that no matter what power a person has in relation to you, there are still boundaries they should not violate.

No matter how understanding your boss seems, you are not his priority. A supervisor who invites confidences, who treats you as a peer, or who leans on you for support is violating a boundary. Your supervisor is not your peer. No matter how much she cares for you and your job, her own job is most important to her. If she has to sacrifice you to keep her position, she will!

Your supervisor's job is to support you as a worker. It is not your job to listen to her problems. If this happens you become her sympathetic ear and your own loyalty becomes divided. Your energy is then diverted from your actual work and a bond is created between you and your supervisor that causes confusion between loyalty to yourself and to the company.

Good boundaries between workers and supervisors and bosses is like good parenting. It allows for safe communication, security in risking, appropriate meeting of needs, attention to role requirements, and support of subordinates. The goal in any business should be the maximum and finest development of the worker.

There's much talk about "flat organizations," "boss-free workplaces," and "egalitarian management." We'd love to believe it, but our experiences with the dark underbelly of the work world has taught us to doubt. Better to err with cynicism and be safe than to let down your guard and be eaten alive.

If you doubt that power differences truly exist, ask who has the power to terminate your livelihood based on a false rumor, or other vague concept such as "competitiveness." Whoever has that clout is NOT your equal. Remember that fact when you are encouraged to "let down your guard, to just be friends." Friends outside; acquaintances inside.

Recognizing Unhealthy Work Boundaries

It is a fact of life that some bosses and supervisors (and even some co-workers) are very unhealthy and abuse their power to get their needs met. If your boss is unhealthy, bullying behavior is woven throughout your organization. If bullying is part of your organization, you have a choice. You can try to develop a healthy base with your co-workers and promote a healthy relationship with your supervisor or boss. However, you might find that as you become more healthy, the people around you will probably resort to more bullying.

Remember if you are asked to cross a boundary that violates your personal space, you will need to assess whether or not this is a healthy place for you to work. You need to ask if you should take yourself out of a work situation where you are being violated or harassed. You should do this as soon as you can. If it is with co-workers, can you practice and use the skills you need to preserve your dignity. If it is with a supervisor or boss, decide whether you can repair the damage to your boundaries. If you can't, you need to look for a new position.

Your Personal Boundary Rights

You have a **right** to privacy. You have the right to choose what questions you answer. You **don't have to** tell anyone your thoughts or feelings. You **are not overly sensitive** if you decline to answer a thoughtless question.

If a boss, supervisor or co-worker seems nosy and asks inappropriate questions you can practice these answers: "I don't feel like talking about it." "I want to keep that to myself." "That's my business." "I'm surprised you think you have a right to that information." "Whoops! That's private."

Chapter 9
Perils of Unattainable Standards

Face your deficiencies and acknowledge them, but do not let them master you. Let them teach you patience, sweetness, insight ... When we do the best we can, we never know what miracle is wrought in our life, or in the life of another.

- Helen Keller

Chapter preview:
The shoulds in our lives
Good news, bad news & expectations
Self-defeating shoulds
Bullying and standards

The Shoulds In Our Lives

A "should" is an internal, private expectation about how the world ought to be. It is our personal standard, the ideal, to which reality is compared. Everything and everyone we encounter is compared to the standard in our head. After a lifetime of judging, the scrutiny is done without deliberate thought. It is automatic.

The internal compass that governs much of our lives is a set of privately-held beliefs and values. There are other forces exerting their influence over what we do and say on a daily basis (a bully is an example of an obnoxious external factor). However, the legacy of our parents is the presence or absence of beliefs that are as broad as a philosophy toward life or that can be as narrow as obsessing over uncrossed handwritten letter "t's" (see the Constant Critic, Chapter 2).

Good News, Bad News & Expectations

The teaching of values and beliefs began in infancy. Attention to our cries was an early sign of respect for us as human beings. Attentiveness rather than neglect molded one of the most primitive attitudes toward others.

We progressed into learning how to handle anger, mistakes, and pain. We learned rules about what is acceptable conversation. Even life goals and the manner in which we treat others were modeled for us or informally introduced by parents and older siblings.

For most of us, parental evaluation of our behavior played a large part in determining confidence or worthlessness. In turn, our values developed from that scrutiny.

Values like commitment, honesty, generosity, dignity, intelligence and a strong work ethic are the parental legacy that ripples through our adult lives.

Kind and ambitious parents were the types to find ways to keep their children inspired. Here's one such inspiring quote.

Aim at the sun and you may not reach it, but your arrow will fly farther than if you had aimed at an object on a level with yourself.

Your childhood experience determines whether you read that statement as a challenge to do even better (with the understanding that you always do well, keep striving to do more) or that your history is one of always taking the easy way out (aiming at a low level) therefore you should take a wild shot at the big prize, though you most certainly won't win.

If evaluations meant anxiety-plagued scrutiny, devastating criticism, and a steady tearing down by your parents, it is no surprise that you, the adult, is paralyzed by fear.

Unfortunately, the world is not populated just by caring, loving parents. In dysfunctional families, children were taught to distrust, attack rather than cooperate, or to lie constantly to cover up family problems.

Deep-seated beliefs can convey a sense of security when they conjure up sweet memories of the time when they were first introduced. Not only are the values important, but the legend of how they were introduced reinforcesthe security.

On the other hand, if chaos is what the child lived with while growing up, there can be little safety in adulthood.

With luck, we acquired a realistic set of expectations about how the world should treat us. We learned to strike a balance between giddy over-optimism and perpetual gloom 'n doom.

The last point we make about the parental role in establishing expectations is that most expectations have a moral tone to them. That is, if you should or ought to be doing something one way, then you had better feel guilty if that is not what you are doing.

The shoulds are also the product of:

- The need to feel **belonging to a group and seeking the approval of others**. The group has tremendous clout over the individual. When a group of co-workers turns on you to side with the bully and they do it uniformly, they put your version of who you are in direct conflict with the one (which is not true) they want you to believe. Most people yield to the group, as incredible as that sounds.

- **Our status in life or our role at work**. People internalize hierarchies in their lives. Different views accompany different levels of organizations in our lives. Husband status activates one set of expectations and wife status creates another.

We take the values and beliefs we learn from our parents to our jobs. If we learned to be overcritical in our Family-of-Origin, then those critical values are the values we take with us to work.

Linda was recently fired from her job as an account representative. She tells her family and friends that she was stupid to ever consider, much less take, this job. She reports to her mother that the job was "demeaning, boring, and unchallenging. I've never met anyone in that line," she says, "who wasn't uneducated and stupid." She vows never to take another job like this. Her opinions are a rationalization created by her need to maintain her self-esteem. She must devalue her job and employer or see herself as a failure.

Shellie works hard at her job, often spending 6-8 hours of overtime per week to ensure that her work is done. She is very vocal in her opinion that one must be completely committed to every job. She states she hates the smallest sign of laziness. However, another way to look at her actions are to con-

sider that she works so hard to only show others that she doesn't need help from anyone. She needs to feel confident and safe and avoid the criticism of others.

In these examples, both Linda and Shellie use their critical beliefs and values to judge themselves in their business lives. Their goals are unattainable, impossibly high with regards to their need for love, safety, and feeling good about themselves. When this happens, Targets need to be more realistic. Often the values that they have been taught have little to do with reality.

Consider Sally. She has graduated from a college that strongly espouses that women are entitled to fulfill themselves personally and through their work. However, she has three strong needs that generate her beliefs about work. The first is the need to win the love of her father who is very critical of her line of work. Her second need is to be able to work and give enough time to her family while she works. A third need is to set an example for her children that both women and men can find fulfillment in work <u>and</u> family. Unfortunately, her needs are in conflict.

Sally has encountered the "tyranny of the shoulds.'" She operates under the principle of the belief that she should be able to be all things to all people (her father and her family), the unforgiving sense of what is right (she should be able to please everyone) and wrong (if she doesn't, she is a bad person).

Why do we do this? We sometimes torture ourselves with guilt and self-blame over things we cannot change. This is why we become paralyzed when we are forced to choose between unbending rules (unattainable or unsustainable expectations) and genuine desire.

Self-Defeating Shoulds

I should

- be able to give to everyone all the time.
- never make a mistake
- be the perfect partner, co-worker, team member.
- never feel hurt.
- always see the bright, positive side of situations.
- always keep my negative emotions under control.
- always be totally self-reliant, never depend on others
- be a complete, multi-faceted life partner.
- anticipate my child's every need all the time.
- never complain about being tired or sick.
- never let the emotions—anger or jealousy—show.
- be respectful and polite to everyone.
- make no enemies.
- never believe I'm good, but wait until others say so.
- always put the needs of others before my own needs.
- never be afraid.
- never make a mistake.

**The Tyranny of Totality Is Self-Defeating
'Always' 'Never' 'Everyone' 'No One'
Can Guarantee Failure, If Not Careful**

Think about it. We all torture ourselves with guilt and self-blame when we are unable to live up to standards that may be too high. We see ourselves as failures. The gap between the way we think the world "should be" for us and our perception of "what is" can generate a sense of worthlessness.

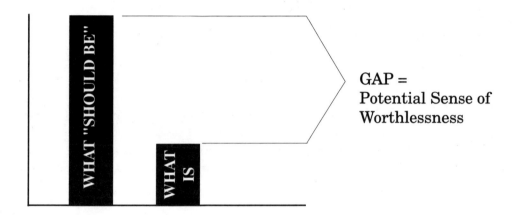

GAP =
Potential Sense of
Worthlessness

Bullying and Standards

The bully's irrational, unrealistic hammering may be reminiscent of tyrannical parents who imposed and enforced martial law while growing up. The emotional cruelty was sufficiently evil. But the longer-lasting legacy is the deeply imbedded belief that you are never quite good enough. That you are always falling short.

Now that there is a bully at work, the parental voices resonate in your mind. It is as if it were yesterday—getting yelled at over trivial matters that "justified" a verbal assault. The bully is the bad parent come home again. As if you needed reminding, you are not a complete individual. The bully thinks her job is to police you so you don't miss an error or shortcoming. This is an outrageous intrusion into your life.

Chapter 10
Your Inner Critic Speaks

The Inner Critic is born during the parental teaching of right and wrong. Later in life, it's that personal, negative, nagging little judge whose attacks are heard only in your head. Everyone has a critical inner voice. Some voices are more strident and demanding than others.

Your Critic

- blames you for things that go wrong
- compares you to others, especially achievements and abilities others have but you want
- sets impossible standards of perfection
- beats you up if you are not perfect
- sticks to a script that describes how you *should* live
- screams that you are wrong or bad if your needs drive you to violate its rules
- tells you to be the best, and if you're not the best, it tells you that you're nothing
- calls you names, leading you to believe they are true
- reads your friends' minds to prove to you that they are bored, turned off, disappointed or disgusted by you

- exaggerates your weaknesses by insisting that you *"always say stupid things,"* or *"always* screw up on the job," or *"never* finish anything on time"

In other words, the inner critic is busy undermining everything you do. If you listen carefully, you might recognize the voice as that of your mother, father or yourself.

The most important thing you need to know about your very special critic is that no matter how distorted or false the attacks may be, *you always believe what is said.* In almost every situation, the critic is there to find fault, blaming and judging you harshly in the process. The critic also reminds you of past failures, connecting them to the present, forever limiting your ability to start anew or to soar with newfound wings.

Our inner critic can be compared with the Freud's superego. The superego is the internalized parent, the moral authority that develops supposedly to hold the pleasure-driven "id" in check. It's the self-righteous, pontificating boorish part of our personalities.

The critic examines everything we do and puts its own spin on it. The critic is always there, whether tearing you down or helping you solve problems and meet basic needs.

Yes, there is a benefit to having an Inner Critic.

Its Purpose

The need to do right

We all have our own values and morals learned in childhood. These serve to create an ethical framework for all activities in your life by defining how to act with family members, authority figures, and friends. The critic helps you distinguish right from wrong. The critic also tells you how wrong or bad you are when you are tempted to break one of the rules.

The need to achieve

The critic helps you achieve goals by whipping you like a race horse. It pushes you along—constantly telling you that what you thought was good is not good enough. It gives you the encouragement to reach goals others might feel are out of your reach.

The need to feel right

Even while the critic tells you you're no good, it helps you by evaluating how you stack up against others. Although it usually finds you lacking, once in a while it will confirm that you are stronger, more attractive and smarter than others. Because this occurs rarely, it reinforces the critic by encouraging you to keep trying to reach unreachable goals.

So your inner critic can both hurt you and help you. The good news is that with practice you can learn to recognize, analyze, and refute the negative destructive criticism while keeping and using what is useful and helpful.

Countering the Critic

You need to be realistic. Face the fact that the most painful criticism of your work might be coming from your own Inner Critic. Most people spend a good portion of every workday bombarding themselves with unrealistically high expectations, while bombarding you with harsh criticisms of the things you don't do well. It is a recipe for feeling like a failure. If you combine this with the critical statements and lies from a bully, you cannot help but feel like you are a failure.

You can improve the way you handle your own Inner Critic. Use the following questions to examine your attitudes toward yourself.

- When you make an error or an oversight at work, do you criticize yourself in a harsh manner?

- Before important meetings, job interviews, or work assignments, are your thoughts negative—do you focus on all that might go wrong?

- When you are running late, do you bombard yourself with harsh criticism, even before anyone else notices you are late?

- Do you worry that you will be found out and that others will discover that you're not really able to what is expected of you?

- Do you lie awake at night criticizing yourself for anything that went wrong during the day, even though you didn't have much control over what happened?

- Have you ever said or thought to yourself that you are your own worst critic?

If you answer yes to even *one* of these statements, your inner critic is working overtime.

If You Invalidate Your Own Hard Work Stop The Self-Destruction Immediately!

Instead of attacking yourself with criticism, take a moment to stop and catch yourself. Ask: "Is this self-criticism necessary and should I spend any time or effort on it?" or "Would my time be better spent getting support and ideas for solutions," or "Does my supervisor's critical nature amplify my own doubts and leave me feeling doubly bad?"

Do not lose sight of all the good work you've done right on a project just because something has gone wrong. Ask yourself if you could address the problem without calling on your own critic. It is also important to keep in mind that you have done a lot of good work that got you this far.

Remind yourself each day or evening of 3 good things you did that day.

Don't remember only the things that go wrong. Avoid focusing only on the things that you can't fix or control. Be good to yourself! At least once a day or at night when you are unwinding from work, take a few moments to acknowledge to yourself (or with a trusted friend) the hard work and worthwhile efforts you did that day. Even on projects that did not turn out as well as you planned, you need to take stock of the valuable planning, thinking, and actions that you've taken that day or that week.

Make sure you don't talk to yourself in a critical manner..

If you notice you tend to talk badly to yourself, stop and say to yourself "I don't need to be so mean to myself or anyone else." and "I don't need to listen to the negative remarks from the bully, I'm doing a good job."

Be aware of an increased susceptibility to be destructively self-critical in certain circumstances. You might try a "thought stopping" technique to disrupt your train of self-defeating thinking. One way is to wear a rubber band on your wrist (hidden under your blouse or shirt sleeve, if you're self-conscious). When the "stinking thinking" starts, simply snap the band. Mindfully switch to another thought. Deliberately get yourself off the negative track. With sufficient practice, you can switch mental gears at will. Then, you can do without the rubber band prop.

Know that the Inner Critic thrives in situations like these:

✓ Meeting new people

✓ When you have made a mistake, public or private

✓ At the start of a new job, project or task

✓ When you feel criticized and defensive

✓ During interactions with management

✓ When you feel hurt

✓ When someone gets angry with you.

Chapter 11
Destructive Mind Games

Chapter preview:
Labeling emotions
Mind games
Reversing the distortions

Initial reactions to a bully's misconduct are typically emotional.

Scientists and philosophers have been speculating for years about what causes bad moods. Certainly there are stories about dysfunctional families and people who suffer from child abuse. However, the Greek philosopher, Epictetus first observed that, "Men are not disturbed by things, but by the views they take of them."

Labeling Emotions

The view that our thoughts, rather than actual events themselves, create our moods has gained acceptance by psychologists, too.

Emotions have two components:
- arousal (physical sensations—gut churning, butterflies, dizziness, profuse sweating, etc.)
- and a label so the mind knows what to call it.

According to this view, we become upset because of the way we *think* about these events. We have the ability to distort meanings related to dramatic events. This ability then helps define our emotional experiences—good and bad.

These distortions, or mind games, weave a protective net that twist and color our feelings according to what we think.

Self-defeating labeling forms the prison walls from which you yearn to break out. The bully brought the bricks and mortar. Through Mind Games, the Target is responsible for the prison's upkeep.

Here's another metaphor. Everyone looks at herself through a telescope. If your telescope is in good repair, you see yourself as important and clearly focused. Unfortunately, most people look through a telescope that is not clearly focused, or it's smudged, or slightly cracked. This blocks the way you see yourself in your life and work and can actually distort your impression of a critical situation.

These distorted thinking styles can make you judgmental and cause you to automatically apply labels to people and events before you get a chance to evaluate them. These distorted labels give you only one side of any situation and cause you to base your decisions on an emotional rather than a rational basis.

You are the only person in this world who can make you feel depressed, worried, or angry. Similarly, you are the only one who can elect not to have these feelings.

If you lose your job, you may feel sad, angry at yourself, or self-critical. Your inner critic starts to whisper in your ear. Your thinking becomes distorted and you may tell yourself that you're no good, that there is something wrong with you. It would be less self-defeating to tell yourself that life is unfair, but for too many Targets, the choice of a label is mindless. It is an automatic process honed over years of practice.

These are Mind Games. They are a natural part of humanthinking. When you *choose* to change the way you think, you can reverse negative, distorted thoughts.

Mind Games

1. **Overgeneralization**. From one isolated event you make a general, universal rule. If you failed once, you'll always fail.

2. **Global labeling**. You automatically use pejorative labels to describe yourself, rather than to accurately describe your qualities.

3. **Filtering.** You selectively pay attention to the negative and disregard the positive.

4. **Polarized thinking.** You lump things into absolute, black-and-white categories, with no middle ground. You have to be perfect or you are worthless.

5. **Catastrophizing**. Worst-case scenario thinking. The danger is that expecting the worst can become a self-fulfilling prophecy.

6. **Personalization.** You assume that everything has something to do with you, and you negatively compare yourself to everyone else.

7. **Mind reading**. You assume that others don't like you, are angry with you, don't care about you, and so on, without any real evidence that your assumptions are correct.

8. **Illusion of Control.** You feel that you have total responsibility for everybody and everything, or feel that you have no control, that you're a helpless victim.

9. **Emotional reasoning**. You assume that things are the way you feel them to be. Others are assumed to have the same feelings as you.

Chris was laid off with several other employees from his company because of a business slowdown. She felt rejected, worried, angry and guilty. Her mind game distorted the layoff as a situation in which she had failed, that the layoff was directly due to her inability to do her work.

Using the Mind Games list, let's analyze Chris' feelings that she is a loser.

- *Polarized thinking:* She's looking at herself in black-and-white categories because she sees herself as a loser.

- *Overgeneralization*: She lost her job, but she is generalizing to her entire life.

- *Filtering*: She is dwelling on her job loss and letting it color her entire view of life. Her choice of husbands is now clearly seen as a poor one.

- *Personalization*: She blames herself for the layoff, rather than the fact that business was slow.

We may say Mind Games are distorting as compared to the perceptions others might have of the same event. However, it is important to remember that there need not be an objective "true" reality. Everyone has their own agenda, perspective and eyes and ears.

The point is that Targets may fall into the trap of undermining themselves with destructive, mental distortions that can slow down or block recovery from the bullying.

Reversing the Distortions

Inside the Target's head

With workplace bullying in mind, note some of the internal monologues you typically hear ...

Now, counter the echo of the bully's words with positive, balanced statements in rebuttal

Try to identify the Distortions, Mind Games

Self-Statement	Distortion	Rebuttal
She's right. Nothing I do is ever accurate. I hate to agree with her, but the job I did on the project was not as good as before.		She's not right! She's just mean. It pleases her to tear into me. Wait a minute. The caliber of my work exceeded that of others then AND now. It may not be perfect, but it is better than this company (agency) has ever had.

Overgeneralization

Filtering

An internal rebuttal like the one above helps defeat the irrational defeatism that plays into the hands of the control freak bully.

Chapter 12
Trapped in Self-Blame

The people who get on in this world are the people who get up and look for the circumstances they want, and, if they can't find them, make them.
- George Bernard Shaw

Chapter preview:
Power of perspective
Bias begets blame
Avoid the trap of self-blame
Internal and external causes: a health risk
Explaining success & failure
Unnecessarily taking blame
Suggested interventions

When you are a bully's Target, there is no doubt that the bully initiated the campaign to disgrace, defame and demoralize you. There is certainty; it is an absolute, undebatable fact. When you tell friends and family, they believe you and stand by you up to a point.

However, others are less supportive or they call you a liar. We mean witnesses, co-workers, the bully's allies, "institutional helpers" (human resources, personnel, employee assistance, legal, ombudsmen, mediators), senior managers, and lawyers.

Yes, it is true that this wildly different version of reality stems from butt-covering (defensiveness), workplace politics, fear, timidity, lack of conscience, and sometimes evil. As strange as it sounds, in their eyes, it makes more sense to see you, the Target, as the cause of your misery rather than the menacing bully.

The lack of support resulting from the myriad of other people's biases further undermines your sanity, increasing the self-doubt you did not deserve in the first place. Heinz Leymann credits this "secondary mobbing" for extending the bad times and postponing recovery from bullying and your ability to move on with your life.

Power of Perspective

We also think it is important for you to understand another factor that explains the madness of blaming the recipient of direct, hateful assaults—Perspective. The perspective we describe is a visual, physical vantage point, not a philosophical one. The determination of who caused what depends a great deal on where one sits.

It's this simple: there are two players in the destructive workplace bullying game—the bully and the Target. If I, as a witness, observe a nasty encounter between the two and am asked to explain why it to turned out the way it did, I have three options:

1. the bully caused it, or
2. the Target caused it, or
3. they jointly caused it to happen

We know from psychological research that the choice of explanations for events depends on a person's vantage point. The phenomenon is called <u>causal attribution</u>. The term attribution refers to the assignment of responsibility to the person, event, process or thing that *caused* the behavior to happen.

Imagine two people seated across from each other in a TV studio. Position three cameras as follows: two peering over the shoulder of each person and aimed directly at the other person (call them bully-cam and Target-cam) and the third recording the situation from the side with both "actors" given equal amount of space in the picture.

We know from research experiments which used such a video set up (though they only recorded conversations, not negative behavior) that observers watching the encounter from the bully-cam, tend to hold responsible the person they see, the Target in our example. These observers have no pre-existing biases, involvement or interest in the taped session and still take the side of the bully in blaming the Target.

To prove the power of visual perspective, other observers, also without bias, hold the bully responsible when watching the encounter from the Target-cam. They literally see the situation through the Target's eyes.

Guess who is held responsible for controlling the direction of the interaction by a third group watching from the side camera? Yes, each person was responsible. In all fairness the researchers dealt with benign conversations, not emotional altercations more likely in the bully-Target pairing. So, an equal split of responsibility would probably not happen. However, the research finding is so strong that we can safely predict some sort of shared responsibility.

Bias Begets Blame

Attributional biases are normal for humans. A person has to mindfully and deliberately fight the power of perspective to be fair. In the bully-Target situation, holding the Target even partly responsible when she did nothing to provoke the bully sounds fair to most observers. But it is unfair to the Target. Calling for "balance," as mediators do, underestimates the bully's role and discriminates against Targets who are the unwilling recipients of indefensible assaults.

As a society, we've had this discussion before. It was about rape victims. Is it fair to fault victims for dressing "provocatively" in the name of balance? That would be the equivalent of seeing the crime from the rapist-cam rather than from the victim-cam. Fortunately, reason prevailed and we have decided to fault the criminal rather than the victim (though the courts and defense attorneys have been dragged slowly to that conclusion). Blaming or denigrating the victim (she was "flirtatious") is showing a compassionless, attributional bias. Until we walk in a victim's shoes ...

So, too, we should stop blaming Targets for their own plight which no one would voluntarily choose.

Avoid The Trap of Self-Blame

As the Targets of most severe bullying tell us, the experience can be as destructive as the complete shattering of one's personality. The Target comes to believe the bully's false story about her. This can happen because the personal attacks are *cumulative*. Regardless of her initial strength, the Target gets worn down.

This is the beginning of the end of self-confidence in one's competence. It's her personal faith in her competence that enables her to confront the bully. When her inner strength is chipped away, the Target is most vulnerable.

Let's extend what we learned about attribution of responsibility to get a peek at how self-destruction happens and what can be done to avoid it.

As far as the delusional bully is concerned, the Target is the reason for the bullying, and those are the words the Target hears from the bully. "You, you, you." (Can't you just see the finger wagging?)

Now switch sides and see the world from the Target's perspective, at least as it should be seen. The bully, operating in a workplace supporting the bully's misconduct is rightfully seen as the cause of the trouble. This is the way attributions normally work. Targets would be biased to blame bullies and the workplace culture that grows them. Bullies would be biased to blame Targets, even without the blessing of an evil personality. It's a matter of perspective, depending upon the angle from which the situation is viewed.

Targets exposed to verbal battering over time, however, mistakenly commit a sort of "reverse empathy." Normally, empathy is a valuable human trait to have—the ability to see the world from the other person's perspective and to share the emotions. In this sick case, it is the Target who sees herself as a defective unit in agreement with the bully.

Siding with the bully actually makes the bully's task easier. The Target inadvertently becomes an accomplice in the tearing apart of her own personality. Too many Targets come to accept the Bully's lies as fact. The campaign of destruction is made easier by the Target's paradoxical cooperation.

We family, friends and co-workers witnessing this self-destruction find it hard to believe as we watch the individual spiral down before our very eyes. There's no objective reason for it, but the process is real. The pain the Target suffers while doing it can be severe. Extensive self-blame may require professional help from a counselor to correct.

Internal and External Causes: A Health Risk

A Target's explanatory style of assigning responsibility is related to mental health. For the sake of the remainder of this discussion, non-Targets will be referred to as "Self-Promoters." They tend to use an attributional bias that keeps them healthy. Call it hubris, vain self-glory, or confidence, they interpret causes of interpersonal behavior differently than do Targets.

Explaining Success & Failure

When explaining their own success (taking a test, winning a job), Self-Promoters generally take credit. They point to either their talent or the effort put into preparation to make the success happen. That is, people usually see success as a result of something about them or some action they took. These causes are *internal* to the person. To credit internal factors means to take *personal responsibility*.

Core internal factors are unchangeable personal characteristics that define who we are. Talent, ability and personality are all internal relatively constant explanations for events. Crediting personality as the reason for success provides quite an ego boost. Change in personality is very hard to accomplish as you know if you've ever tried a major self-improvement campaign. (Changing someone else's personality is a recipe for misery—yours.) Your personality's stability, its constancy, is crucial to living an organized, chaos-free life.

Effort fluctuates with circumstances. Sometimes you prepare or rehearse hard, sometimes you do not. With each opportunity, comes the chance to do it differently. Effort is internal, but changing.

	CONSTANT	CHANGING
INTERNAL	Intelligence, Talent	Good Effort, Motivation

Of the two internal sources of success, intelligence is preferred by most people because internal, stable causes are more predictable. Better to do well because you're smart than to have put forth a good effort.

When it comes to explaining failure, Self-Promoters (non-Targets) prefer *external* factors. External causes include the difficulty of a task. Why did the Self-Promoter fail the test or not get the job? She may reason, it "did not test for the important things"; "they hired only 1% and they all had friends on the inside." If no plausible explanations come readily to mind, the Self-Promoter points to bad luck, "it just wasn't my day."

Applying the same categories of constancy and changeability to external factors, the range of possible explanations (attributions) for events is complete.

	CONSTANT	CHANGING	
INTERNAL	Intelligence, Talent	Good Effort, Motivation	≺ Preferred for Success
EXTERNAL	Difficulty/ Ease of Task	Fate, Bad Luck	≺ Preferred for Failure

To blame external factors for failure is technically ducking personal responsibility.

Attribution theory and the therapeutic approach that evolved from it are more about mental health and wellness than finding fault or fixing blame as a moralist would dictate. Moralists have a political agenda. Don't confuse the information they disseminate in a public arena with solid advice that has helped people recover from life-damaging events like bullying.

The Positive Mental Health Bias
Success: Take Personal Credit
Failure: Blame Something 'Out There'

Unnecessarily Taking Blame

It is instructive to study depressed individuals and their explanations for why things happen. Bullied Targets are often depressed. Their pattern of explaining events is exactly the reverse of normals. Failure is blamed on internal factors. One can beat oneself up for not trying hard enough (the internal effort explanation), but even the depressed person can be made to see that there will be other chances to try harder in the future.

However, when a person sees her personality as hopelessly flawed or defective, it is the strongest type of self-inflicted attack possible. That is what depressed people do. Their self-loathing somehow seems justified in their mind. All negative thoughts and lost confidence begin with the assumption that the person is irreversibly screwed up. It's not easy to escape from a pit like that.

In the same self-defeating manner, success is discounted by crediting external forces. "I passed only because it was an easy test" "I got the job because the interviewer was unskilled" "I was lucky."

"Cognitive therapy" with depressed people attempts to reverse self-defeating attribution. Restoring self-confidence requires the person to see that the core of her being has a solid, positive foundation. In addition, the person has to be taught to look for environmental factors that can account for, even if only partially, personal behavior.

Here's how the table of explanations works for self-defeating Targets. The rows are swapped with the Self-Promoters' preferences. That is, success is discounted and minimized. Failure is taken on the chin, which is an unnecessarily harsh disrespectful approach.

	CONSTANT	CHANGING	
EXTERNAL	Easy Task	Dumb Luck	⊰ Preferred for Success
INTERNAL	Stupidity, No Talent	Poor Effort Low Motivation	⊰ Preferred for Failure

Now relate this to being an unwitting Target of a series of bullying verbal assaults. The heart of the attacks is the lie that the Target is a worthless human being. This is not true and the Self-Promoting person knows this. Over time, doubt can creep into the minds of even the strongest. If the bully is shrewd (and most bullies are), she will use subtle lies that are offensive only in their repitition. This wears through the Target's defenses.

Part of the bully's effectiveness in disrupting the lives of other people is her ability to create chaos. Making statements that run counter to the reality everyone shares in a workplace certainly is the manufacture of madness. If the bully gets away with keeping everyone off balance so that no one can predict the next assault's timing or content, the bully achieves the control she desperately seeks.

Working in a chaotic, assaultive place can wear down the defenses of the "strongest" people. It is difficult for Targets to be close-minded, even when it comes to hearing the bully's pathological view of the world.

Bullies Win When Targets Accept Personal Criticism As If It Has A "Kernel Of Truth" In It

By somehow justifying the fit between lies and reality, the Target begins to let the bully define a darker reality for her. The actual person gets lost in the translation. [If you want to fundamentally change who you are, don't let the bully define your goals for you. Make 'em butt out!]

Finally, we witnesses see evidence that the self-blame process has taken hold. Successes are discounted or explained away. Setbacks are internalized, with a disproportionate amount of responsibility taken for events that were completely out of the Target's control.

In other words, the bully can goad the Target into adopting a depressed person's perspective. Then, shortly thereafter, genuine depression sets in.

Suggested Interventions

Targets and their loving family and friends need to be aware of how attribution works. By recognizing the shift to explaining success outside themselves while blaming themselves as the sole source of failure, others can intervene to stop a Target's downward spiral into depression.

If it is you who is experiencing the mental and emotional shift, get help from a counselor *now*. Your awareness about how this happens will speed your recovery. Keep a written record of your thoughts, explanations and feelings after events. The pat-

tern of self-blame should become evident. You will have to deliberately re-train yourself to take credit for success and let
failure roll off your back in order to get strong again. This may
sound vain, but recovering from trauma requires dramatic corrective steps.

Ignore instructions from others about taking "personal responsibility." You did nothing to bring on the assault from the
bully. Take responsibility for shutting out the bully's lies; ignore others who side with the bully. Their advice is not good for
your mental health, for your survival. The bully wants to steal
your dignity at work. Appropriately explaining your actions is
a first step toward reclaiming that dignity.

If it is someone you love who is going through the early stages
of self-destruction, avoid at all costs agreeing with the dysfunctional explanations you hear her utter. You have to counter the
person when she or he says they are defective, no good, a total
loser, etc. It sounds easy, doesn't it? How could you not resist
the lies yourself?

Over time, the bully can penetrate the psyche of the strongest, most optimistic person alive in an attempt to "convince"
her that she is wrong. Eventually, dealing with wounded Targets challenges the staunchest supporters. Do not listen to lies,
be a constant booster of the person's competence. Give specific
examples. Don't simply say "you are a good person." Instead
say that "volunteering to tutor immigrants in English is worthwhile and the students love you for it, they say so."

Finally, let a professional counselor help you help the Target if either you or she gets in too deep.

Chapter 13
Denial of Needs and Wants

Chapter preview:
Fundamental, basic needs
Needs vs. wants
Wants inventory
What your inventory says
Clarifying what you want
Rules for requests

After working through the preceding chapters, you now have the tools for minimizing emotional devastation by the bully. Now we will help you define your own needs and wants, suggesting ways to recognize the difference between them. By doing so, you can begin to practice before your next encounter with the bully. At some point, you will have to confront the bully, to make it clear that her unacceptable, inappropriate behavior must stop.

The Target's Declaration Of Needs & Wants Signals The End Of Targethood To All Past & Future Bullies

Fundamental, Basic Needs

We all have legitimate needs—environmental conditions, activities, and experiences important for physical and psychological health.

Too often, Targets forget that they are entitled to having certain basic needs met. Needs are absolute rights to which every human being is entitled. During bullying episodes, when the bully's lies convince Targets that they are worthless, needs are ignored. Sadly, some Targets come to believe that they must relinquish their needs.

The following list has examples to remind you about what you need in life. You may think that some of the needs don't apply to you at all, or that there are needs you feel have been omitted. Feel free to add or omit the needs based on what is important to you.

Physical needs
- clean air to breathe
- clean water to drink
- nutritious food to eat
- clothing and shelter
- rest and enough sleep
- exercise
- physical safety, freedom from harm

Emotional needs
- to love and be loved
- to have companionship
- to feel respected
- sympathy and compassion from others
- to reciprocate that sympathy & compassion
- when you do well—recognition & appreciation
- when errors are made—forgiveness and understanding

Intellectual needs
- information
- stimulation
- challenge of solvable problems
- variety
- time for recreation and play
- to grow and to change.
- freedom to honestly express your thoughts
- authentic, consistent responses from others

Social needs
- to interact with others
- to be by yourself
- work, not necessarily a "job"
- a role in society that helps define an identity through which you make a positive contribution to others
- to feel that you belong to a group
- to not have confidences broken by group members

Workplace needs
- employer-provided resources to do the work
- accomplishment of tasks free from interference
- consistent application of internal rules & policies
- compliance with governmental regulations
- work environment free from health hazards
- freedom from retaliation if civil rights are exercised
- a psychologically stable workplace culture
- privacy with respect to matters unrelated to work

Spiritual, moral, and ethical needs
- to seek meaning in your life
- a way of putting a value into your life
- compliance with a higher moral code

My Fundamental Basic Needs

Use the following worksheet to list your unique needs:

Physical Needs . . .

Emotional Needs . . .

Intellectual Needs . . .

Social Needs . . .

Workplace Needs . .

Spiritual, Moral, Ethical Needs . . .

Other Important Needs

Needs vs. Wants

The important distinction between needs and wants is that needs comprise the necessary basics for living. Quality of life depends on going above and beyond fundamental needs. Wants reflect wishes.

For many Targets, it is hard enough to ensure that others honor and satisfy needs. One shouldn't have to beg for the basics. Bullies who violate a Target's rights also deny basic needs. When feeling passive, vulnerable and assaulted, it is almost unthinkable for a Target to believe she also deserves to have her wants satisfied.

Ask yourself: Do you ignore your less vital needs and wants if they conflict with someone else's? Do you often identify essential needs as "extras" and neglect them? If you do, then you forego your own comfort. Would others do the same?

You have a right to have your needs met. At the same time, you need to recognize that you deserve to have wants met as much as anyone else. You do not need to be stoic or a martyr. You are just as important as anyone else.

Sometimes you might absolutely *need* to talk to a co-worker about an aspect of your job. At other times, the job problem might seem less pressing and you *want* to discuss it, but you can postpone working on it until later.

You are the one, the only one, who can judge the importance of your needs and wants. If it is important to you, *you* have a right to ask for it. No matter what anyone else thinks!

The following exercise can help you identify wants that you desire, but were afraid to ask for. They are divided into three parts:

(1) what you want,

(2) who can help satisfy your wants, and

(3) situations in which you would ask for what you want.

Wants Inventory

Go through the list twice.

First pass: place a check beside all items that apply

Second pass: rate the checked items on this 3-point scale:

1 = Mildly Uncomfortable
2 = Moderately Uncomfortable
3 = Extremely Uncomfortable

WHAT

I have trouble asking *FOR*:

- approval for
- help with certain tasks
- someone to listen and understand
- work evaluations
- promotions or raises
- respect
- time by myself
- answers to my questions
- permission to make my own choices
- acceptance of who I am by others
- acceptance of my mistakes

other: _____

WHO

I have trouble asking for what I want *FROM:*

- my husband/wife/partner
- fellow workers
- clients
- strangers
- friends
- acquaintances
- my boss at work
- sales people and clerks
- authority figures
- a group of more than two or three people
- a person of the opposite sex

other: _____

WHEN

I have trouble asking for what I want *WHEN:*

- I want help
- I ask for service
- I need a favor
- I ask for information
- I want to propose an idea
- I feel guilty
- I feel selfish
- I ask for cooperation
- I negotiate from a one-down position
- a lot of people are listening
- others' tempers are high
- I'm afraid of looking stupid
- I'm afraid the answer will be "no"
- I might look weak

What Your Inventory Says

Look over the inventory. Notice the things you want the most, the people from whom you want them, and when it is most difficult for you to ask for what you want. Look at the patterns that emerge. These are most likely the people and situations in which you need to acknowledge you feel less confident. List the problem areas in order of their rating and their importance to you.

Clarifying What You Want

After you have identified the wants important to you, formulate an assertive request. If asking for things is hard for you, prepare your requests in advance. By preparing an assertive request first, you can get the facts and relate them to others in a clear and concise manner. The clearer you are, the less the bully can pick you apart.

Use the following guide to prepare your requests.

From _____

Write the name of the person who can give you what you want. If there are several people from whom you want the same thing, write out separate requests for each of them.

I want _____

> Spell out what you want the other person to do. Stay away from abstractions like "show respect" or "be honest." Don't ask for a change of attitude, instead, specify an exact behavior: "I want an equal vote in deciding the new overtime policy."

*When*_____

> Specify a deadline for getting what you want. Give the exact time of day you want someone to do something, or the frequency with which you want something—use any aspect of time that will provide you a time table and won't allow for any misunderstanding. For example: "I would like to have my review the Friday following my 3-month probation."

*Where*_____

> Write down the places where you want something. "Please give me one half hour alone at my desk in the morning to organize my day."

*With*_____

> Specify any people connected to your request. "I would like to meet with you (the supervisor) and Sue (the co-worker) when you decide what shifts we will have next month."

Rules for Requests

1. Try to get the other person to agree on a convenient time and place for your discussion.

2. Keep your requests small to avoid resistance from the bully.

3. Keep your request simple, one or two items will be easiest for the bully to remember.

4. Don't attack the other person. Use "I messages" so you can stick to **your** thoughts and feelings. Remember to be objective and stick to the facts. Keep your tone of voice moderate.

5. Be specific. Don't hedge when you give exact times and figures for what you want. Focus on asking for behaviors, not a change in feelings or attitude.

6. Use assertive words and high esteem body language. Maintain eye contact, sit or stand straight, uncross your legs and arms, and make sure you speak clearly, audibly and firmly.

7. Practice, practice, practice! Stand in front of the mirror to observe how you look when you request what you need. This will allow you to correct poor posture or to practice confident facial expressions.

Once you have determined what you want to say and how you will say it, you will be ready to face the bully at work. Start with a small request. Build one success upon another. Progress steadily through your list of wants, from the modest ones up the list to the most desired.

You need to work on your requests until they are clear, direct, and as positive as you can make them. Remember, the satisfaction of your needs and wants does not come at the expense of others. You are asking for no favors; your are simply claiming that which is your right.

Practice with friends and trusted co-workers to make sure you have asked for what you truly want.

PRACTICE CLARIFYING WHAT YOU WANT

FROM . . .

I WANT . . .

WHEN . . .

WHERE . . .

WITH . . .

When ready, go take on the bully.

Chapter 14
Anger and Shame, Emotions of Bullying

Anger: The Mask

The experience of bullying brings strong feelings. If you are like the majority of Targets, your feelings are expressed as anger. But the problem is not about anger.

Anger is always the cover for another emotion. Lurking beneath the surface, waiting to be "outed" and confronted, is the real issue. It could be hurt, disappointment, jealousy, fear, shame, frustration, guilt, or some other emotion.

All emotions have two parts:
- arousal (physical sensations—gut churning, butterflies, dizziness, profuse sweating, etc.)
- and a label so the mind knows what to call the experience.

Anger is the wrong label. To stomp away in a rage from an encounter with the bully serves only to postpone a confrontation by the Target about the resentment felt when previously assigned projects are re-assigned to a less competent co-worker in order to humiliate the Target in front of her co-workers. If the Target stays angry and never confronts, the golden opportunity to reclaim her dignity and self-respect vanishes in a cloud of unnecessary emotion. The bully fears most being held accountable for her illogical cruelty. An angry Target allows the bully to duck responsibility.

A Gallup poll conducted in the summer of 1998 for the Marlin Co. found that 42% of the 800 workers surveyed felt at least a little anger at work. The scale ran from not at all angry to extremely angry.

As Targets know, bullies are sources of stress (stressors) and anger. We prefer to lobby against anger because it postpones a Target's recovery.

Anger is an index of the toxicity of a poisoned workplace. We have to quit blaming individuals entirely. Instead of searching for the perfect personality test to predict which individuals are most likely to be angry, those who care about workplace health should search everywhere at the company for people who enrage others and set off anger for their personal viewing delight. Bullies "burn people" much like arsonists love to watch conflagrations of their making.

Investigators and reporters see workplace anger as a malady inherent in disloyal, crazy employees from whom prissy senior management (aka "leaders") must be protected.

The obvious alternative is to eliminate anger by eliminating the source of the devastating emotions that the workplace creates, which drive people to hide the pain beneath a mask of anger.

Anger Is The Target's Enemy

Some indicators that you are angry.
- flushed skin
- shallow breathing
- clammy skin
- rapid breathing
- tearfulness
- loud voice
- jitters
- light-headedness
- tensed muscles
- loss of concentration
- bulging veins

Anger can be turned inward and become self-destructive.
- Do you overeat?
- Overdrink?
- Overwork?
- Have you allowed yourself to become so stressed that you have trouble working and functioning adequately at home?
- Do you blame yourself for everything that goes on around you?
- Do you rage at your partner or children?

Sadness and feelings of loss often lie beneath anger. This happens when people are afraid of showing emotions of vulnerability. Anger, the more "socially acceptable" emotion, sometimes masks sadness. Some stereotypes are invoked. Men should not show emotion; women show too much "soft emotion." Anger is the great equalizer.

People are afraid of anger itself, too. Unresolved anger causes the bearer pain. Many people carry their anger for years but are not aware of it.

Some people are afraid of any intense emotions. Anger scares them the most. They worry about consequences if they express their anger. Sometimes anger erupts with disastrous results—harming not only those who hold the anger, but their co-workers, partners and children. The violent expression of anger is destructive, nonproductive and essentially ineffective. Violence hurts; it doesn't heal.

The perception of anger as destructive comes from childhood and the Family-of-Origin. Many children, faced with their parents' anger feel that the anger is directed at them. These children feel helpless and overwhelmed. They want to disappear.

To them, the parents are angry and raise their voices because of something the child did. Whether or not this is true or logical, it is how the child feels. This fosters the idea that somehow the child is at fault. It is taken as a personal attack, even if not intended that way. Anger destroys the beginnings of self-esteem and feelings of self-worth. If the parents don't make a special effort to clarify why they were angry, the child often anticipates the worst. She assumes responsibility for the parents' emotions.

As an adult, the grown child feels that if she disagrees with someone, if she needs to say no to someone, if she raises her voice in anger, that that anger will hurt someone just as she was hurt by her parents.

This perception needs to be corrected. We all have times when we raise our voices. We all need to say "no" once in a while. We need to disagree. However, these incidents do not need to be a destructive. Certainly no one should dread disagreement or being different.

Anger can also be a very constructive energy. To be constructive, it needs to be worked through and released. The goal is to let go of the anger, not to collect and hold it. The first step in letting go of your anger is to own it, to acknowledge that anger is the best name for what is felt inside. Unresolved anger accumulates over time and eventually eats away at your soul.

Although no two people are exactly alike in managing their anger, experts on anger have defined five general ways anger is dealt with. These are: (1) suppression, (2) open aggression, (3) passive aggression, (4) assertiveness, or (5) dropping your anger. The first three tend to perpetuate anger. The last two can lead to success.

Suppressing Anger

Because so many Targets have witnessed the destructive effects of anger, they hesitate to admit their own anger. They vow not to be lowered to emotions that seem overbearing or crude. They never want to appear rattled or weak, so they maintain a cool exterior of being above all problems associated with anger. When confronted with anger, they want to appear emotionless and pretend to feel no tension. They express surprise that anyone would assume they might be angry.

Most Targets who suppress their anger believe that anger is bad, that expressing it will cause them to be seen in a negative light. Holding in anger is the only way they know how to interact with others.

Look over these statements to see if you hold in your anger.

____   I am afraid I will look bad if I let others know my problems.

____   I tend to become resentful of others although I don't want others to know.

____   If I am flustered, I tend to keep it to myself.

____   If a co-worker upsets me, I tend to let days go by without mentioning it.

__   Sometimes I am frozen when faced with an un-wanted situation.

__   I avoid having conversations about sensitive top-ics.

__   I frequently suffer from headaches and stomach upsets.

If you checked 3 or more of these statements, you are very good at suppressing your anger.

Targets have been trained to think that anger is not nor-mal. They have been invalidated when their perceptions are different than others. They fear retaliation if they express dis-agreement with others. However, suppression of anger only causes feelings of failure and personal defeat.

Open Aggression

For many people, anger brings a mental picture of open aggression. They picture anger as taking a stand for personal worth and needs that comes at the expense of someone else. This anger brings images of explosive rage, intimidation, and blame. However, it is not limited to such violent pictures. It also includes bickering, criticism, and sarcasm. This type of anger springs from a focus on personal needs rather than a sensitivity to the needs of others. Open, overt aggression is public.

Review the following list to see if you practice open aggression.

__   I can be blunt and forceful when someone does some-thing to frustrate me.

___   As I speak my convictions, my voice becomes increasingly louder.

___   When someone confronts me about a problem, I am likely to offer a ready rebuttal.

___   No one has to guess my opinion; it is known by everyone.

___   I overlook others' feelings because I focus so sharply on fixing the problem.

___   I am likely to argue with my family members

___   When in an argument with someone, I tend to repeat myself.

___   If I think someone else is wrong, everyone knows.

___   I give advice, even when it is not solicited.

If you checked 5 or more of these statements, you probably have a pattern of open aggression.

Passive Aggression

Targets who vow not to become rageful when they are angry recognize that open aggression creates a hostile environment. They refuse to explode loudly or get into a debate with a bully. They feel that it is destructive to disagree. It is to be avoided at all costs. This leads to passive aggression which involves expressing anger in a manner that preserves personal worth, needs, and convictions at someone else's expense.

The following list has examples of passive-aggressive anger. Check the items that apply to you.

___   I use silence to let others know when I am frustrated.

___   I tend to sulk and pout.

___   I procrastinate when I do not want to complete a project.

___   I will never admit if I am frustrated. Instead I will lie and pretend everything is fine.

___   Sometimes I avoid others so they won't bother me.

___   Sometimes I will deliberately ignore others when they try to talk to me.

___   I avoid face-to face conversations.

___   Sometimes I do things behind others' backs.

___   Sometimes I do things to others to irritate them.

If you check 5 or more items, you show the tendency to express your anger in such a way that you succeed in putting limits on your anger. But you are only communicating anger in such a way that will cause you further tensions and stress.

Assertive Anger

Anger defined as preserving personal worth and personal needs while also considering the needs and feelings of others represents a form of anger that truly helps relationships to grow. It shows maturity and personal stability.

It is important to distinguish between assertiveness and aggressiveness. In the past, assertiveness was often confused with pushy and abrasive behavior.

Assertiveness is not mean and is not meant to harm others. It allows a Target to address personal concerns about her self-worth, personal needs, and leaves the door open to conversations about differences between the Target and the bully.

The following are examples of anger expressed in a non-hostile assertive manner.

- When overworked, you can firmly and politely say no when asked to do even more projects.

- When in charge, you can state project goals without resorting to harassment or being bossy.

- When overwhelmed by work, you can request help from co-workers without threatening retaliation if old "no."

- You can tell your boss or co-workers that you will take your lunch break and not answer the phone or solve any problems during that time.

- With co-workers you can talk about differences and offer advice without raising your voice or altering your tone of voice.

To learn how to express assertive anger you need to remember two main points:

1. Make sure you expend your emotional energy on subjects that matter and concentrate your attention on matters that are not trivial, and

2. Learn how to distinguish when you use tone of voice to convey your anger.

Remember that assertiveness is not always the easiest thing to learn. It takes time and practice to be able to manage your anger.

Dropping Anger

The hardest decision to make is the choice of letting go of your anger. There are times when you desire to communicate without anger and you use your best assertive voice, but you still become locked in an angry debate with a bully. At this point, you have the option to choose to drop your anger.

Dropping your anger means you recognize your personal limits. You accept the inability to communicate with the bully. This choice allows you to walk away from the frustration and hurt that the bully created.

Dropping your anger also indicates that you have accepted the fact that your anger control does not depend on someone else. However, you must remember that dropping it is not suppressing it. Suppressing your anger is only an exercise that will leave you with unresolved feelings of hurt and bitterness.

A Final Thought About Anger

Reasonable responses to situations that cause anger are responses that help you maintain your cool and put the situation into your control, not to yield control to the bully.

Here are some ways to release anger:

❏ Re-establish your boundaries

❏ Use active listening to communicate your willingness to understand any problem

❏ Calmly tell the person that she is the source of your anger

❏ Exercise by running, walking, working out, or swimming

❏ Lie on your back and do scissors kicks with your legs

❏ Throw back your shoulders and arms as you say, "Get off my back"

❏ Talk to friends, family or a professional or all of them to sort out your feelings

When you take responsibility for your feelings and emotions, you are released from the bond that ties you to the bully and the continual feeling of inadequacy. You choose to take care of yourself, rather than to use the bully's actions to continue the destructive pattern of mistreatment.

Shame

If you have been bullied, you will experience shame. The shame might be slight, but in many cases it is overwhelming.

It is important for a Target to understand that shame is not guilt.

**Guilt Is What You Feel When You *Make* A Mistake
Shame Is What You Feel When You *Are* The Mistake**

Shame is a very painful feeling and is the result of the incorrect feeling that there is something inherently wrong with who you are. Shame is the gut-wrenching feeling that you are bad, inadequate or defective.

After three years as a personal assistant to the vice president of her company, Pat lost her job. Her boss, Mary had always been critical of Pat's work. Pat had tried her best to please Mary, working overtime and redoing projects when Mary complained that they weren't up to the company's standards

After months of her boss's torment, Pat lost her temper and screamed at Mary. The result was a corrective interview and Pat was fired three weeks later.

Pat felt shame when she lost her job. She told herself, "I'm no good. I'm worthless, and I'll never get another job."

For Pat, the pain of her harassment dominated all her thinking. Shame came over her in waves. Her sense of unworthiness became so strong that no matter what others said, she was convinced she was flawed.

Many families use shame to control others. Careless parents make statements such as, "All you ever do is lay around" or, "You're going to be a bum, just like your father" "You'll never get a job; you have no skills" and "Oh, Susie, you'll never get in a college, your grades are not good enough."

Targets raised in families with shame carry that shame from childhood into their adult lives. When you are raised in a shame-based family, you don't know any other way to act. It's easy to understand how Pat might think, "I can't find another job, I'm just no good." Shelly, unemployed for ten months, truly believes she is a failure and reminds herself of this every morning as she looks into the mirror. These two women have retained the shameful messages of childhood and continue to reinforce them.

To Heal From Shame

Feelings of shame are the natural consequences of bullying. Healing from shame involves breaking the silence of pain. When you encounter a bully and you recognize that you feel shame:

- contact past co-workers and ask them to remind you of your past good work with them

- as you listen to the positive feedback you get, take time to let in the message that you are a good and competent worker

- identify the shaming messages you have internalized and the hurtful events you have experienced

- separate what is unreasonable and untrue from who you are

Hurtful events and messages that have been internalized need to be challenged. You need to be able to say; *that's not about me! It's not about my worth or identity. It hurt me terribly, and it has caused pain in my life, but it's not about me. Shame is not my identity, I am a good and worthy person.*

As you put your feelings about shame into words, as you identify how bad you feel, you will be able to let go of the shame and move on with your life. The more you talk with others you trust, the easier it will be to let go of the bad feelings. The more you acknowledge that the bullying isn't really about you, the closer you will be leaving the bully behind.

Section Three
Moving On, Up or Out

BullyBusting
(If it were only like this)

Chapter 15
BullyBusting

What counts is not necessarily the size of the dog in the fight, but the size of the fight in the dog.

- Dwight D. Eisenhower

Chapter preview:
When you dare to challenge Goliath
Readiness
Advice from bullying war veterans
Preparation for getting the bully off your back
Tribunal checklist

When You Dare To Challenge Goliath

We have found that the effect of bullying on Targets follows a very predictable pattern. There are ups and downs and lots of switching directions in mood and energy.

There are two reasons for being aware of the emotional cycle you're likely to experience. The first advantage is that you will be less surprised. In a Target's chaotic world, any predictability is useful. Let's review the stages before talking about the second benefit.

1. Victimhood

The immediate pain of harassment (and the physical pain from your psychological injury) dominates all thinking. Too easily forgotten are the 20 years experience you brought to the job.

We guess that the harassing manager was new to the job or your unit. How could this have happened to me? you think. It's easy to feel beaten as you research your options and learn the destructiveness of the effects of bullying. People without the experience are incredibly naive about rights and procedures. The adversarial employer offers no information that gives you an advantage. Oddly, those who have gone before you rarely offer advice, somehow thinking it best for you to discover the tortuous by yourself.

> ***Cure:*** Know it is the system that creates or sustains a creepy, malicious person like the abusive bully. You were not singled out based on any real flaw or weakness. That means you're a nice person. Attackers simply prefer less combative victims.

2. Power Surge

Help is found! The Workers' Compensation/Disability/EEO complaint systems are discovered. Tales of favorable jury awards or large settlements in cases like yours suddenly appear. Attorneys are found, though not carefully screened (you will be able to write a book about this topic within a year). With friends and advocates, you actually feel sorry for the wrongdoing employer. You are all-powerful. Sure, you hear warnings about how long justice takes, but at this early stage, the future looks rosy.

> ***Cure:*** Hold onto these feelings. You'll need the strength. As you repeatedly hear the merits of your case and how much you deserve to win, let the rationale sink in. You'll need to hear the echo to get you through stages 3 and 4.

3. Vulnerability

The counterattack begins by the employer. Their side begins to show how deep their pockets are. Their resources are limitless compared to your puny contingency-based lawyer's office. Your lawyer stops returning your calls because, after all, she has PAYING clients. There is a steady stream of interrogatories (questions from the company counsel) leading up to the dreaded deposition. If your case goes that far, your lawyer's percentage also rises.

Depositions are institutionalized assassinations. You're never quite ready for the experience. Just remember corporate lawyers believe in a "scorched earth-no survivors" strategy. Your lawyer probably didn't have the time to rehearse you completely for the inquisition. To listen to the employer's defense arguments, you begin to feel like you should apologize for working for 20 years and hampering their productivity for so long — you ungrateful, incompetent, greedy, sleezeball!!

Of course, if you are not suing in a court of law, the HR bureaucrat in charge of minimizing workers' comp claims for the employer—someone you probably knew as an acquaintance while working there—becomes the enemy. Your needs directly conflict with her job security. These auditing types have few friends at work because distrusting others ("they all file fraudulent claims") is central to doing their job well. Yucky people.

Personnel is now squarely on the employer's side. Because you have an injury, you begin to learn firsthand how much access employers have to your medical records. They review your prescriptions. Had a temporary depression after your father's death? They've got records that will be misconstrued to impale you. You are a worthless piece of dung and hooked on doctors and drugs. Pain? You'll be labeled a "chronic pain patient"— code for illegitimate pain. Now the descriptions by physicians come to be used against you: spinal disk enlargement, not uncommon for a person your age, soft tissue damage is undetectable, pain is subjective, no treatment exists, you'll just have to work through it, and surgery is not advised. Stress is a mental fiction.

> *Cure:* Keep telling yourself it is the other side's job to fight back. Keep your mind on the justice you seek. Watch legal shows on TV (Court TV, Rivera Live) to see how adept defense lawyers are at rationalizing what they do on behalf of corporations. Also you might get an idea or two for your lawyer on strategy. Read Ralph Nader's book *No Contest* to validate your fight.

4. Isolation/Abandonment

Now you feel alone. The other side has shown its muscle, and it is scary. Your white knight attorney now seems weak and fades into the background. Colleagues from work, former friends, find it hard to keep in contact. They fear being in your place someday and treat you like you have the plague. It is ironic that it was they who encouraged you so strongly to stand up against the cruel manager, but did not do so themselves. You imagine them on the stand testifying against you at a trial.

> *Cure:* Refuse to be alone. Force friends to maintain contact. Take the initiative. Join or start a support group of targets of harassment at work. Stay involved with life outside your case. Volunteer to help a group do something you've always wanted to do. Start the at-home business you've longed for. Be your own boss. Don't let the dispute become your life's defining moment; shove it into the background. Don't lose the passion for your case, simply throw your day-to-day energy into constructive activity. Build or make something. Get involved with something or someone.

Don't let all family discussions drift toward progress on your case.

Tell your story to a reporter. Renew old relationships with friends who knew you before this fiasco and who did not work with you. You deserve validation that you indeed had a life before. The current dispute does not define who you are as a person. Write the case details down and your feelings. Get therapy to deal with the downside of challenging a big bad employer.

5. Anger

It is usually aimed at everyone, primarily yourself, but even at supporters. Partly because you are no longer in your regular work routine, with time on your hands and isolated, the vengeful arguments directed at you from the other side can begin to make sense. This is very dangerous. Don't let the "kernel of truth" in. Self-doubt feeds on itself, relying on the script written by your enemies.

Cure: Read books about how to defuse anger. It is too destructive to turn it inward. It is antisocial to rage at others. Trust your sense of self defined by those who love you rather than to focus on garbage from the other side of a legal fight.

6. Resolution

You find a way to move on. In victory, you can become a Forgiver of enemies more quickly than in defeat. At the end, partly to make sense of the stressful process just endured, you could become a Crusader. You fought for a cause and find that many others have the same plight. You want to help. There may not be a business in it for you, but you feel fulfilled doing meaningful work. You forget that you ever worked for that crummy employer.

> *Cure:* Moving on while allowing resentment to fade is the most certain path to your positive mental health and feelings of self-worth. Winning a lawsuit does not necessarily give the sense of closure on this darkest chapter in your life. What seems to matter most is registering your disgust at the bully's conduct and letting her, the company, the world know that you found it outrageous and intolerable.

One woman who suffered under a bully for years decided to complain, to fight Goliath. She passed through all the phases. Her resolution was the delight she felt the day she waved goodbye to her tormenter as the bully left work forever, preferring to take early retirement rather than stay and fight. No headlines, just a long-postponed quiet victorious moment as the bully was banished.

South African Susan Marais-Steinman and Magriet Herman, authors of *Corporate Hyenas At Work*, wrote about the wisdom they had gleaned from surviving retrenchment (reorganization, downsizing) and its accompanying traumatization. Like us, they saw a multi-step process of an indeterminate length for Targets to fully and finally resolve the dilemmas in their lives that bullies create. Similarly, they describe stages that look initially like endings but prove to be part of the middle.

Their Road to Recovery phases are:
1. *Bewilderment* — disbelief, a sense of unreality
2. *Akuna Zinkinga* (Zulu term for "there is no trouble") — the first window of relief

3. *Moment of Truth* — time for realistic assessment of personal strengths and weaknesses and planning to regain control over your destiny — perhaps the longest phase
4. *Mourning* — facing the reality of loss
5. *Turning Point* — the decision stage — choosing to either withdraw from life or to rejoin life
6. *New Life* — on balance, the positives outweigh the negatives — you feel Hyenawise (BullyProof in our terms) — empowerment — won't be fooled again
7. *Free At Last* — no longer can anyone steal the potential you are born with

Readiness to Confront

The second advantage you get from knowing that your moods will go up and down over time is that you can more accurately determine your "readiness to confront." When you do finally decide to stop the rationalization (for whatever reason—perhaps at the insistence of your heart doctor), it is critical that you have enough stamina to see the fight through to the end.

If you commit too early, at the early Power Surge stage, you will come crashing down, relatively unprotected, while your attorney dawdles and fritters away time.

Little children cannot be potty trained until their biological clock says all the organs are ready. In a similar fashion, no confrontation should be undertaken until you are psychologically stable. Because self-doubt plays such a major role in bullying, it is important to be genuinely confident that there is nothing wrong with you before you begin the fight that will expose any remaining vulnerabilities.

You cannot effectively fight alone, nor be motivated to win unless you are somewhat angry. Anger is on the other side of hurt. Stop the hurt first. Then, fight if you want to. Readiness pertains to both legal and informal challenges to the bully and her support cast of managers.

Should you fight at all? This is a very personal decision. Here's advice from some of those who have been there.

Advice From Bullying War Veterans

Here is wisdom, in their own words, from Campaign survey respondents who were asked to say what would they have done differently when bullied:

> *Take a stand and get the help you need to confront the bully, because you wouldn't have a bully on your back if there were more people on your side.*

> *Fight back from the beginning*

> *Realize that the bully is really a coward ... Also realize that you should not back down, but don't become a bully yourself*

> *Tell others that you trust what is happening. Build support and get ready to confront. It is not okay! Reflect on your past work experiences and realize that this is related to the bully and not truth about you. Constantly do reality checks with others.*

> *Don't take any kind of crap from anybody. Stand up to them.*

> *I think I did the best thing by confronting him. I also provided support to others who were being annoyed by his behaviors and encouraging them*

to speak up. I also informed my senior colleagues of his behavior and its effects on me ... that was a tremendous help...they had been putting up with it and sloughing it off...when they realized that he was hurting me and [they] even heard some of the comments and thought them "stupid," they intervened by giving friendly advice to him.

I would have challenged the bully more and stood up for my own beliefs instead of backing down.

I would have confronted the situation earlier, taken legal action, and been less passive and forgiving.

I would have gone to the operations of our corporate office or the district manager with my complaint instead of our immediate manager.

I would have kept a better record of bullying incidents

As you can see, the message is confront rather than face certain ongoing humiliation.

It is better to die on your feet than to live on your knees.
- Dolores Ibarruri

If you decide to fight legally, you'll have to consult an attorney. But if it is reasonably certain that the law provides no protection, we offer our method of BullyBusting.

BullyBusting is a process that you coordinate because you are your own best advocate.

Do Not Attempt BullyBusting Unless & Until You Are First BullyProof

Preparation for Getting the Bully Off Your Back

- Identify allies: yours and the bully's. Safely test the loyalty of each. Watch your backside.

- Ask for support AND action from your allies, poll others to gauge the extent of harm.

- Solidify support from family and friends outside work.

- Know why co-workers and "Institutional Helpers" (HR, EAP, Attorneys) rarely help. File complaints with them only with minimal information. Save your best info for your lawyer.

- Research the law and the organization's own policies, documents, mission, vision, values, policies & procedures, annual reports, etc. Search for violations committed by the bully. If you plan to threaten to sue, consult an attorney first.

Schedule Two Meetings

(1) **With senior management** one or two levels above the bully. Alone with that person (or in a group if a group is being bullied) point out economic costs to the organization of tolerating bullying. Estimate the costs of stress (workers' compensation, disability), lost customers, lost productivity from sick days, turnover costs, legal fees for the employer, setttlement costs, and the intangible price of lost reputation in the community, etc.) Downplay emotional consequences. Get a promise of immunity from retaliation for you and testifying witnesses. Have the manager agree to discipline or terminate the bully when evidence presented at the second meeting proves that the misconduct violated laws or internal codes. Ensure that person's attendance.

(2) **The Tribunal** (kangaroo court) at which the bully is confronted with the unacceptability of her actions. She goes on trial in a court you arrange and direct. Notify witnesses and the senior manager when and where. Put human resources on notice to attend to ensure compliance with any existing disciplinary procedures.

Tribunal Checklist

1. Announce the meeting to all participants separately (no disclosure of the distribution list to the bully) with the stated purpose of reviewing the performance of the bully.

2. Hold the meeting at a site neutral or adverse to the bully.

3. Have clearly defined, specific outcome expectations. What do you want? Bully transferred? Monitoring of the bully?
    Ensure protection against retaliation, direct or indirect.

4. Record the meeting with deliberate redundancy (in case one set of records mysteriously disappears). Have audio and written records or written and video.

5. The confrontation is to showcase the bully's unacceptable actions against fellow employees, any relevant impact on customers, clients or team members, any discovered violations of organizational policies, or laws broken. It is NOT a recitation of emotional impact.

6. You, as the Target, provide testimony as do other witnesses
    - first, review the charges of policy violations
    - have witnesses testify & bully gets chance to respond

7. Close the meeting with all parties signing an agreement (a contract) that prohibits further mistreatment of the Target by the bully. Sanctions or termination should be the consequences for the bully when subsequent violations are reported. Produce with a laptop computer and printer on location.

8. Ensure written permanent immunity from retaliation and protection from future harm. Have the senior manager warn the bully for all to hear.

Chapter 16
When Enough Is Enough

The soul of man is immortal and imperishable.
- Plato

Chapter preview:
Stay or go
A quiet exit
The Work Doctor alternative

Stay or Go

We end the book where most Targets begin, with a question. "Should I quit and run?"

The Campaign Survey Says . . .

75% of Targets Stop Bullying Only by Leaving

Bullies stay, Targets are driven out

Only you know the answer. Only you know how low the quality of your work and personal lives have fallen as the result of bullying.

You get no medals for "hanging in there." Look back to Chapter 9 and see if toughness is one of those unattainable personal standards that you believe you must meet.

We suggest doing a cost-benefit analysis on a two column sheet. Look at the differences in both quantity and quality of the items in each list to make your decision. Leaving a job is a private decision to be made only by you and your life partner. Do the required math yourself.

Sacrifice Health & Sanity For A Paycheck? It Simply Doesn't Add Up

For what it's worth, we coach people as long and as hard as we can to get them to do some BullyBusting before giving up. However, the kiss of death for potential BullyBusters is when the bully has support all the way to the top of the organization. Targets facing unanimous opposition like that do not stand a chance. If no allies can be found above the bully, you'll never gain the leverage against her that you need to get her out.

If the workplace is a convenience store and the bully is a co-worker but the owner hired her, polish your resume and hit the road.

A Quiet Exit

There are literally thousands of traditional career counselors out there to advise you about leaving gracefully. They can tell you how to transition to the next job without ruffling feathers. To summarize their approach: burn no bridges, kiss the behind of the bully boss so she won't say bad things about you, never be negative (which we guess means to be truthful) about the job-ending turmoil you are leaving behind when interviewing for the next job, smile and put your future in the hands of those who have ruined your life to date. That is alternative #1.

The Work Doctor Alternative

We suggest a slightly different approach—alternative #2. It involves guile, cynicism and paranoia. But the bully pushed you into this mess in the first place. Never forget that.

✓ Record, if possible, all meetings and documents that the bully-zealot had the audacity to dump on you. Employers now do genetic screening of blood samples without job applicant's knowledge. They plant surveillance devices throughout the worksite to "protect their property." There is no explicit right to privacy. Courts always question whether or not the person watched or recorded had the "reasonable expectation" of privacy. In the workplace you should expect that the employer's property would be considered public (except for toilet stalls, and even then, there seems to be some doubt).

If you are considering doing something stealthy, call the Privacy Rights Clearinghouse in San Diego — (619) 298-3396. Additional contact information may be found at www.bullybusters.org.

✓ Pursue legal or EEOC complaints, if applicable. Your departure is imminent when complaints are filed. As a rule, retaliation is swift, severe and persistent for those who dare to complain.

✓ Arrange for positive references from colleagues, allies up the chain, and customers who will verify that your performance record was impeccable. You need people to confirm in writing that you are a skilled competent person. If the next employer is more obsessed with your subordination and willingness to sell your soul to a tyrant than your talent, would you want to work there anyway?

✓ Know the law regarding defamation of character. Goad the bully into defaming you to others. Get it on the record. (Most bullies will actually boast of the smear campaign they launch against you.)

David Hurd, attorney and author of the *California Employee Survival Handbook*, states that it is illegal for an employer to make a "misrepresentation which prevents or attempts to prevent a former employee from getting a new job...A misrepresentation can include any act, suggestion or inference that leads the listener to believe something untruthful or misleading... (even) gestures, or tone of voice, or a raising of an eyebrow could qualify as an illegal misrepresentation." Proof can be provided by DRC. See the fourth following suggestion.

According to Hurd, if an employer "volunteers to another person or another employer, the reason or reasons, for an employee's discharge or reason for quitting-that employer is guilty of a crime ... The past employer is only permitted to disclose the truthful reasons for the discharge or voluntary termination of the employee if the past employer is specifically asked without prompting."

✓ Write your own letter of recommendation and make the employer sign it before you leave. Even if they hate you, just maybe their fear of confrontation will convince them to sign. Plus this might balance the practice of making you sign forms against your will (such as stating that your departure was voluntary to cut you out of unemployment benefits). Then you can threaten them with legal action if they renege on the letter or choose to state anything more than employment dates if and when contacted. If they go along with this letter, you can skip the next suggestion. Move to DRC to verify compliance.

✓ Deliver a letter from an attorney representing you (pay for 1 hour's time) to the employer in a way that proves receipt. The letter warns all those listed that they, as individuals and the company, will be held liable for the release to future employers any information prohibited by law regarding your employment at the company.

✓   If the employer insists on an "exit interview," use the opportunity to deliver one or more of the letters prepared. You are leaving. So, you control the meeting agenda for once. Be prepared for gestapo-like tactics.

✓   Because warnings don't stop liars and cowards, consider using a unique pro-employee service from DRC (Documented Reference Check (800) 742-3316) The company calls your ex-employer as do future post-bullying employers checking your references.

Since they are working for you, for a modest fee, DRC transcribes exactly what is said about you. Then the defaming statements give an attorney ammunition to exact your pound of flesh from them for continuing the bullying after you're gone. Using this service doesn't stop them, but it might help you get a settlement from them large enough to cushion the economic blow from being "constructively discharged" from the job you once loved.

✓   Worst-case scenario. You might have to launch a pre-emptive strike at a job interview if no letters were signed as suggested above. Prospective employers are always desperate to talk to your ex-employer. Tell them there was conflict and positive news from the bully is not likely. If you then let them know how you expect to be smeared, then you will have "self-published" the defamation you anticipate. According to Hurd, your statement would be admissible in court to show you have been defamed by disclosing the false statement made against you by the ex-employer. Direct their attention to the positive comments from others whom you can trust.

Admittedly, this sounds like hardball, but doesn't that describe accurately how the employer and bully conspired to mistreat you? It's an alternative to the quiet exit.

Why? Because Work Shouldn't Hurt!

Appendix

The Campaign Against Workplace Bullying
Survey

Labor Day, 1998

Three online surveys were posted at the web site as part of the initial research of, and for, bullied workers. Targets of bullying had been invited to complete part one, the <u>Target</u> survey, and part two, the <u>Aftermath</u> survey, to describe some of the consequences of bullying that have lingered. A third survey for <u>Witnesses</u> of the bullying of others was designed for co-workers.

The initial 200 completed surveys were analyzed. The summary of our findings appear below. In all, 154 Targets and 46 Witnesses completed surveys. Sixty-six Targets also completed the Aftermath questionnaire.

Though the sample of respondents does not represent a randomly representative group, thus rendering the study a "non-scientific" one, it is a look directly into the belly of the beast which too many of our sick workplaces represent.

Bullying was defined at the web site as the hurtful, repeated mistreatment of a Target (the recipient) by a bully (the perpetrator) whose actions are characterized as controlling.

At time of publication, data collection continued at the web site, www.bullybusters.org. Updates and revisions may be found there.

Gary Namie, Ph.D.
Coordinator, Campaign Against Workplace Bullying
Managing Partner, The Work Doctor

Major Findings

1) <u>Bullying is different</u> from the more recognizable issues that plague the workplace — sexual harassment, racial discrimination and violence. Both women and men are victimized as Targets and serve as perpetrators.

2) Falling prey to a bully's destructive tactics is <u>a career hazard</u>; it is not about gamesmanship or a fair competition among equals. Bullies commonly adopt surprise and secrecy to gain leverage over Targets.

3) <u>Targets are a diverse group</u> of normal, talented people.

4) <u>Bullying devastates</u> the Target's emotional stability and <u>can last a long time.</u>

5) The <u>employer, as an organization, bears partial responsibility</u> for the systematic disassembly of a once productive employee by a mean-spirited one-person wrecking crew.

Detailed Findings

1) <u>Bullying is different</u> from the more recognizable issues that plague the workplace — sexual harassment, racial discrimination and violence. Both women and men are victimized as Targets and serve as perpetrators.

It is a type of harassment that ignores the legal condition of disparate treatment based on gender. Female Targets were nearly equally likely to be bullied by women (46%) as men (54%). Though men were a minority of the respondents (27.2%), they, too, were bullied. For them, the bully was usually male (72% of the time). Legality is not required for acknowledging its existence.

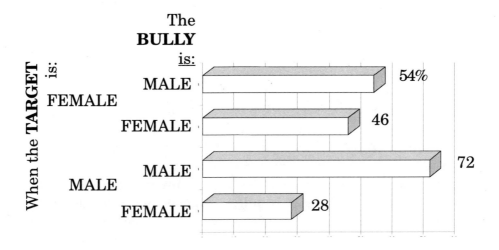

The **BULLY** is:

When the **TARGET** is:

FEMALE
- MALE — 54%
- FEMALE — 46

MALE
- MALE — 72
- FEMALE — 28

Furthermore, less than 10% of the respondents felt that legal charges could be brought against the bully based on EEOC (Title VII) criteria—gender, race, etc.

Bullying is unconscionable meanness and a precursor to violence, if left unchecked. It is limited to verbal assaults and sabotage. Results confirmed this in that in only 6.5% of the cases were physical threats made.

2) Falling prey to a bully's destructive tactics is <u>a career hazard</u>; it is not about gamesmanship or a fair competition among equals. Bullies commonly adopt surprise and secrecy to gain leverage over Targets.

What exactly did bullies do? The top 10 tactics ranked from most to least frequent were: blame for errors, unreasonable demands, criticism of work ability, inconsistent application of made-up rules, threats of job loss, insults and put-downs, discounting accomplishments, social exclusion, yelling and screaming, and stealing credit for Target's work. Bullies all adopted more than one spirit-crushing technique. Witnesses tended to see making unreasonable demands, stealing credit, blaming and threatening job loss as bigger problems than did Targets themselves.

The top four causes of the bullying, as seen by Targets and witnesses, were: a refusal to accept the subservience the bully sought (A-31%), "bully envy" of the Target's competence and abilities (B-21%), nothing known since the assaults were unprovoked (C-18%), and top-down company policies, the workplace culture (D-14.3%). If bullying was a civil interaction, independence would be rewarded instead of having attack as a consequence. Bullying is as capricious and surprising as the bully's personality is unpredictable.

Targets' Rationale For Being Bullied

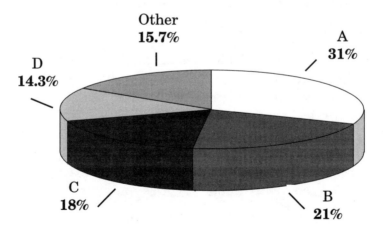

Most important was that three out of four (75%) of those who reported that bullying had stopped said it did so only because they left the job. Terminations were engineered by bullies with falsified facts or without bothering to concoct a reason (which is rarely illegal). Others quit after being driven out. Bullies stay; Targets leave.

The bullies' favorite arena for misconduct was in public in front of others (53.2%). Public actions not only humiliate the Target but serve notice to the group that anyone could next fall into the predator's crosshairs. The other half of the bullies divided their preference between private, truly secret settings (24%) and encounters behind closed doors but overheard (22.8%). Privacy enables deniability. Disputes become a "she said/she said" dialogue which discourages people to whom the Target turns for help to not take remedial action.

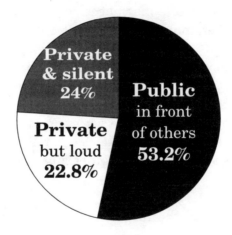

3) <u>Targets are a diverse group</u> of normal, talented people.

Targets and witnesses who completed the surveys were predominantly female (73%). The age range was 15 to 58, with a mean age of 36, and 78% of the respondents between the ages of 24 and 46.

Education: 43% had less than a 4 yr. college degree; 27.5% have a 4 yr. degree; 29.5% have a graduate or professional degree.

Most employers were in the private, for-profit sector (59.3%); 15.4% were nonprofit organizations, and 25.3% were government employees.

Typical employers: legal office, toy manufacturer, aerospace, chamber of commerce, private elementary school, casino, physician's medical group, substance abuse counseling center, big 6 accounting/consulting firm, national magazine, university, community action agency, state prison, hospital, semiconductor manufacturer, software design, bookseller, satellite communications, resort hotel, pharmaceuticals, pipeline construction, book publisher, market research, chiropractor.

Representative jobs: "a checkout chick, a register dog," nutritionist, professor, janitor, training officer, corrections officer, machinist, researchers, beverage supervisor, fraud investigator, heavy equipment operator, tech support, clinic director, engineer, child care worker, nurse, bank teller, teacher, purchasing, security officer, design engineering, sales, quality control assistant.

4) <u>Bullying devastates</u> the Target's emotional stability and <u>can last a long time.</u>

As rated by Targets, the list of most prevalent 8 effects bullies had on Targets were: stress, anxiety (79.4%), depression (64.7%), exhaustion (64%), insecurity, self-doubt (59%), shame, embarrassment and guilt (58%), obsessive thinking, nightmares (58%), poor concentration (56%), and sleeplessness (53%).

Those who completed the Aftermath survey were evenly divided into two groups. The shorter-term group was removed from their bullies for one year or less. A second, longer-term group had a "recovery time" that spanned 18 months to 10 or more years. The short-term group reported frequent or constant intrusive negative thoughts about the bullying in 81.25% of the cases. This alone is horrific.

More disturbing is that 23.5% of respondents in the long-term group were bothered by frequent or constant thinking about the bullying. Remarkably, for those removed from the bullying for 10 years or more, 80% said they "sometimes" still thought about it.

Subsequent to the bullying episode to which respondents referred in their questionnaires, 58% reported that they were still troubled by bullying (that it was either an infrequent or debilitating part of their current job). Freedom from bullying is obviously difficult to achieve once wounded.

These data confirm the anecdotal evidence we gather as part of our advising service.

5) The <u>employer, as an organization, bears partial responsibility</u> for the systematic disassembly of a once productive employee by a mean-spirited one-person wrecking crew.

The bully's rank in the workplace was higher than Target's in 89% of the cases. Of the others, 6.7% were co-worker bullies and 4.5% bullied up the organization chart.

Recall that the fourth-ranked perceived cause of bullying was the employer's culture (top down policies). Further support for the employer's condoning, rather than condemnation, of bullying came from the question asking who supported bullies. Management was the principal source of support (76%) while the bully's peers ranked second (56.3%).

Sadly, the Target's co-workers were seen as pro-bully, though at a level less than half that of management (32.4%). This could reflect the success of a "divide and conquer" tactic that bullies sometimes adopt to turn co-workers against peers. The final noteworthy supporter of bullies was Human Resources, according to 30% of survey respondents.

Who Supports the Bully?

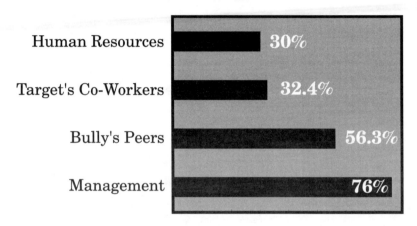

When asked to rate the helpfulness of company representatives, the two least helpful were Human Resources (an average of .423 on a scale of 0 to 2, and only 3% saying they were helpful) and Senior Management (an average of .424 and 7.6% crediting them as helpful).

Witnesses tended to discredit HR and Management more harshly than did Targets, though the differences were not statistically significant. It is reasoned that, as outsiders, they saw more objectively how the Target's downward spiral could be attributed to HR and Management's indifference or deliberate obstruction of a compassionate resolution on behalf of the Target.

The question of responsibility for bullying was raised by having respondents distribute 100% of accountability across four groups. The average percentage assigned to Targets for their own fate was 8.2%. Bullies bore the brunt of responsibility, an average 59.5%. However, the organization was given an average 24% and the law (society or unknown external factor) was assigned slightly more culpability (8.3%) than Targets. Clearly the bully and her accomplice, the organization, were seen as the culprits.

Targets Divide the Responsibility for Bullying

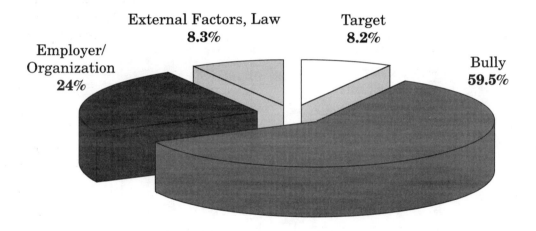

Again, witnesses tended to view the bully more harshly than Targets (64.5% vs. 58%), but the difference was not significant.

Some good news about co-workers came from the list of sources of support for Targets. Co-workers topped the list, but co-workers saw themselves as more frequently supportive than did Targets (95% vs. 72%). Next most supportive as seen by Targets were friends away from work (62%), a spouse or partner (58%) and family (51%). Note how friends are consulted more frequently than mates. We infer that the shameful nature of assault victims drives them to shield loved ones rather than burden them first.

Who Supports Targets?

Percentages reported for groups

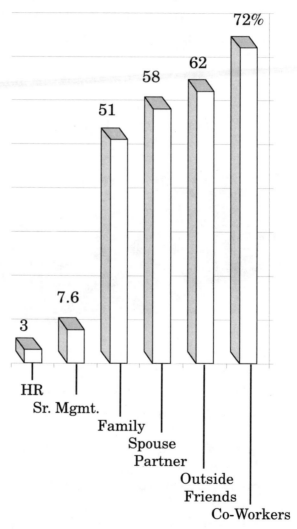

Management provided the least support to Targets (8.5%).
Management loyalty is showered on bullies.

Bibliography

Bach, George & Deutsch, Ronald. *Stop! You're Driving Me Crazy.* G.P. Putnam, 1980

Brown, Stephanie. *Safe Passage: Recovery for adult children of alcoholics.* John Wiley & Sons, 1992.

Frank, Robert H. & Cook, Philip J. *The Winner-Take-All Society: Why the few at the top get so much more than the rest of us.* Penguin, 1995.

Harvey, Jerry. *The Abilene Paradox and Other Meditations on Management.* Lexington Books, 1989.

Hornstein, Harvey. *Brutal Bosses and Their Prey: How to identify and overcome abuse in the workplace.* Riverhead Books, 1996

Hurd, David J. *The California Employee Survival Handbook* (3rd ed.). Pro Per Publications, 1998.

Keashly, Loraleigh. (1998) "Emotional abuse at work: Conceptual and empirical issues." *Journal of Emotional Abuse*, Vol 1.

Levine, Daniel S. *Disgruntled: The darker side of the world of work.* Berkley Boulevard, 1998.

Marais, Susan & Herman, Magriet. *Corporate Hyenas At Work: How to spot and outwit them by being hyenawise.* Pretoria, South Africa: Kagiso, 1997.

McCarthy, Paul, Sheehan, Michael, & Wilkie, William. *Bullying: From backyard to boardroom.* Alexandria, NSW, Australia: Millennium Books, 1996.

Nader, Ralph & Smith, Wesley. *No Contest: Corporate lawyers and the perversion of justice in America.* Random House, 1996.

Neuman, Joel H. & Baron, Robert A. (1998). Workplace Violence and Workplace Aggression: Evidence concerning specific forms, potential causes, and preferred targets. *Journal of Management*, Vol. 24, pp. 391-419.

Privacy Rights Clearinghouse, Dale Fetherling (Ed.). *The Privacy Rights Handbook: How to take control of your personal information.* Avon Books, 1997

Schaef, Anne Wilson & Fassel, Diane. *The Addictive Organization: Why we overwork, cover up, pick up the pieces, please the boss & perpetuate sick organizations.* Harper & Row, 1988.

Solomon, Norman. *The Trouble With Dilbert: How corporate culture gets the last laugh.* Common Courage Press, 1997.

Tobias, Paul & Sauter, Susan. *Job Rights & Survival Strategies: A handbook for terminated employees.* NERI, 1997.

Index

If after reading this book, you want Personal Coaching
from the authors, call 707-745-6630
(9-5, California time)
for a telephone appointment.

The Personal Coaching Service is available as:
- a single, crisis-stopping session, or
- on a regularly scheduled basis

Ask for the discounted prepaid
Personal Coaching Service.

A prepaid PCS account makes a wonderful gift
for a bullied friend.

ABOUT THE AUTHORS

RUTH NAMIE, PHD

Ruth is the Support Services Coordinator for the Campaign Against Workplace Bullying, the non-profit organization she co-founded. Dr. Namie has been a psychotherapist since 1986 with a doctorate in Clinical Psychology. She maintains a private practice in Benicia, California and facilitates support groups for working women. She also has experience as a corporate Training Director in retail human resources management and in the Hawaiian hospitality industry. She created training programs for employees and managers. It was her personal experience with bullying that led to Campaign services and publications.

Ruth and Gary have been married 16 years.

Gary is a social-organizational psychologist. He brings experience as a manager, project & management consultant, management professor, steelworker, driving instructor & pizza man. He was professor of management and psychology at 12 universities at graduate & undergraduate levels. Since 1985, he's worked on everything from aircraft cockpit redesign to Quality (tqm) to public program evaluation. He has delivered hundreds of seminars, courses and speeches on every imaginable workplace topic. He is National Coordinator, Campaign Against Workplace Bullying.

GARY NAMIE, PHD

WORKSHOPS, SPEECHES, ON-SITE PROGRAMS AVAILABLE
707.745.6630 FOR INFORMATION

Join the Campaign Against Workplace Bullying!